dustry Canada
esearch Publications Program

PERSPECTIVES ON NORTH AMERICAN FREE TRADE

MODELLING LINKS BETWEEN CANADIAN TRADE AND FOREIGN DIRECT INVESTMENT

By *Walid Hejazi amd A. Edward Safarian*
University of Toronto

Aussi disponible en français

Canadian Cataloguing in Publication Data

Hejazi, Walid, 1963-

Modelling Links between Canadian Trade and Foreign Direct Investment

(Perspectives on North American free trade)
Text in English and French on inverted pages.
Title on added t.p.: Modélisation des liens entre le commerce et l'investissement étranger direct au Canada.
Includes bibliographical references.
ISBN 0-662-64134-5
Cat. no. C21-28/3-1999

1. Investments, Foreign – Canada.
2. Canada – Commerce.
3. International trade.
4. Free trade – Canada.
5. Canada – Economic conditions, 1991-
I. Safarian, A. Edward.
II. Canada. Industry Canada.
III. Title.
IV. Series.

HG4538.H44 1999   332.67'3'0971   C99-980118-XE

The list of titles available in the Research Publications Program and details on how to obtain copies can be found at the end of this document. Abstracts of research volumes and papers published in Industry Canada's various series, and the full text of our quarterly newsletter, *MICRO*, are available on *STRATEGIS*, the Department's online business information site, at http://strategis.ic.gc.ca.

Comments should be addressed to:

Someshwar Rao
Director
Strategic Investment Analysis
Micro-Economic Policy Analysis
Industry Canada
5th Floor, West Tower
235 Queen Street
Ottawa, Ontario
K1A 0H5

Tel.: (613) 941-8187
Fax: (613) 991-1261
E-mail: rao.someshwar@ic.gc.ca

TABLE OF CONTENTS

PREFACE

Toward the mid-1980s, as international markets and production were becoming more global in scope and outlook, Canada was in danger of being pushed to the margin of the world economy. We were not equipped to expand our participation in global markets, and we were in danger of losing our own markets. Moreover, with over two-thirds of our exports destined for the United States and the share steadily climbing, we were highly exposed to rising U.S. protectionist sentiments. In essence, our past prosperity had made us complacent about the precarious position we faced as a trading nation.

It was in such a climate that the government undertook the steps necessary to renew and strengthen the economy, rather than resist the forces of global change. The government's approach was to make the private sector the driving force of this economic renewal. Policies were adopted to encourage and reward entrepreneurship and facilitate adaptation to the changing economic environment.

As a trading nation, getting our trade relations with the United States right was an obvious goal. It was decided that a free trade agreement was needed in order to forestall protectionist tendencies in the United States, enhance Canada's security of access to the American market and improve the predictability of trade relations with our neighbour to the south.

The Canada-United States Free Trade Agreement (FTA) was implemented in 1989. Five years later, in 1994, the North American Free Trade Agreement (NAFTA) came into effect and basically extended the FTA to the fast-growing Mexican market.

These free trade agreements were expected to increase prosperity in Canada by raising the efficiency and productivity of Canadian businesses. Such agreements are known to be mutually beneficial to the economies of the parties involved, and are particularly beneficial to the relatively small economies, such as that of Canada. They first expose domestically protected firms to international competition. Second, they reward innovative and productive firms by giving them access to larger markets. This increases trade flows between participating countries and improves the overall efficiency of their economies. The FTA and NAFTA were no exception; they were signed in the hope of obtaining those benefits for the Canadian economy after an initial adjustment period. Yet concomitantly, there were legitimate concerns about possible plant closures and job losses in Canada.

More than ten years have passed since the implementation of the FTA — enough time to reliably assess the implications of the agreement for the Canadian economy. In this context, the Micro-Economic Policy Analysis Branch has asked a group of experts to examine the Canadian economy in light of the FTA. The six papers coming out of this exercise are now being published under the general heading of *Perspectives on North American Free Trade*. These papers analyse a broad spectrum of issues ranging from the impact of the FTA on interprovincial trade flows to its impact on the productivity performance of the Canadian economy. In addition, the viability of the Canadian manufacturing sector is assessed, as is the relationship between outward foreign direct investment and trade flows. The papers also explore the implications of trade for the evolution of Canada's industrial structure and skill mix along with an assessment of Canada's migration patterns with the United States.

To date, most of the research on the impact of foreign direct investment (FDI) has concentrated on the domestic implications of FDI in Canada. It is often noted that FDI is an important source of international technology transfer and, hence, of economic growth. The study by Walid Hejazi and Ed Safarian addresses the issue of FDI from a different perspective. It looks at the impact of outward FDI on the economy, and more specifically on exports. The authors dispute the commonly held view that outward FDI transfers production facilities from Canada to other locations and causes reductions in Canadian export and employment levels. Contrary to popular belief, they document that Canadian outward FDI is complementary to trade. That is, increases in outward FDI will lead to increases in Canadian exports.

The authors also examine the inward side, measuring the link between FDI coming into Canada and its impact on imports. They find that increased levels of inward FDI are also associated with increased imports into Canada, but that the size of the impact is only one-third that of outward FDI on exports. Thus, they conclude that increased outward and inward FDI have a positive impact on Canada's trade balance.

EXECUTIVE SUMMARY

A common view is that increases in outward foreign direct investment (FDI) substitute for domestic exports. Similarly, increases in inward FDI result in lower imports. However, recent evidence implies that FDI and trade may not in fact be substitutes for one another, but rather complementary. Using bilateral trade and FDI data between Canada and 35 other countries over the period 1970–96, this paper establishes that trade and FDI are complementary. This is done within a gravity model framework. The analysis is extended to the industry level (SIC-C 1980) for which bilateral FDI data are available. The authors show that the links between trade and FDI vary substantially across industries.

1. INTRODUCTION

Foreign direct investment (FDI)[1] has played an important role in the Canadian economy for many years. Canada, however, has typically had more inward FDI than outward FDI. In 1980, the ratio of inward FDI to GDP was 21 percent. Although this ratio has remained stable over the period 1980–96, there has been a marked increase in outward FDI. The ratio of outward FDI to GDP was only 9 percent in 1980, but jumped to 22 percent in 1996. That is, Canada now has about the same outward FDI as inward FDI.[2] These trends are presented in Figures 1 and 2. Such observations raise important questions. In particular, what have been the implications of such increases in outward FDI on the Canadian economy?

Most research with regard to Canada has concentrated on the host country implications of FDI; in particular, it is often assumed that FDI is an important source of international technology transfer and thus economic growth for the host economy.[3] Relatively little attention has been given to the impact of outward FDI on the home country (Canada). This paper measures one important: its impact on Canadian exports. We feel that any discussion of the consequences of outward FDI for the Canadian economy must at a minimum consider the impact such FDI has on Canadian trade as an input. Only by understanding this relationship can we begin to have a good idea of the link between FDI and domestic welfare.

We use a gravity model to measure the link between outward Canadian FDI and Canadian exports on a bilateral basis to thirty-five countries over the 1970–96 period. A common view is that outward FDI transfers production facilities from Canada to other locations thus reducing Canadian exports and employment levels. We argue that this is not necessarily the case. In particular, to the extent that FDI is a complement to trade, increases in Canadian outward FDI will cause increases in Canadian exports. This is indeed the result we document. We undertake a similar study on the inward side, measuring the link between FDI into Canada and imports. We find that higher levels of inward FDI stock increase imports into Canada, but that the size of this impact is only one third that of higher outward FDI on exports. One interpretation of these results is that higher levels of outward and inward FDI have a positive impact on Canada's trade balance.

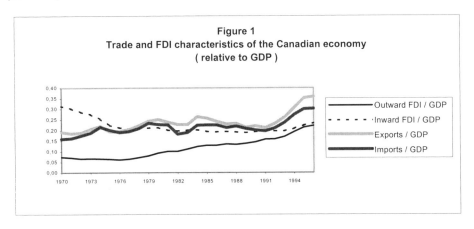

Figure 1
Trade and FDI characteristics of the Canadian economy
(relative to GDP)

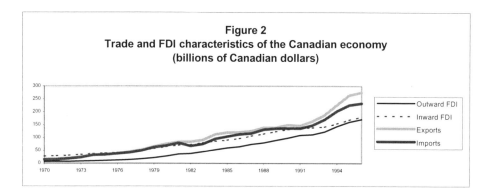

Figure 2
Trade and FDI characteristics of the Canadian economy
(billions of Canadian dollars)

Canadian outward FDI may transfer low-wage, low-skill production to other countries, and at the same time increasing in the production of high value-added goods to be exported, thus causing an increase in high-paying, high-skill jobs in Canada. In other words, it may be the case that higher outward FDI in one industry causes exports to increase in other industries. That is, even if one finds the intra-industry relationship between trade and FDI to be one of substitutes, they may be complements when considering inter-industry links. This therefore motivates extending the analysis to the industry level.

We have put together comparable trade and FDI data at the industry level between Canada and the United States and United Kingdom on the outward side, and between Canada and the United States, United Kingdom and Japan on the inward side. Since there are so few countries, it is not possible to estimate a full gravity model to measure the links between trade and FDI at the industry level. To undertake such an analysis, we would need the industry level data between Canada and several countries at the industry level.[4] We therefore estimate a much more limited model at the industry level for 13 industries.

For the outward regressions, we find the link between exports and outward FDI to be positive in 9 industries and negative in 4. For the positive industries, 3 are statistically significant. For the negative industries, 3 are also significant. In particular, exports and outward FDI are found to be complementary in chemicals, chemical products and textiles, construction and related activities, and accommodations, restaurants, recreation services and food retailing. There is a negative or substitution relation in machinery and equipment, transportation equipment, and communications. For the inward regressions, we find the link between imports and inward FDI to be positive in 10 industries and negative in 2. For the positive industries, all 10 are statistically significant. For the negative industries, 1 is significant. In particular, imports and inward FDI are found to be substitutes only in transportation equipment and in electrical and electronic products. Surprisingly, however, these industry level results do not seem consistent with the aggregate regressions, perhaps owing to the preliminary nature of the industry level regressions. We therefore put more weight on the aggregate regressions.

The format of the paper is as follows. Section 2 reviews the literature. Section 3 gives a description of the data. It includes a discussion of the aggregate data as well as the industrial distribution of Canada's trade and FDI. Section 4 examines the theoretical links between trade and FDI and section 5 provides empirical estimates of these links. Section 6 gives a discussion of possible welfare effects, and section 7 presents our conclusions.

2. LITERATURE REVIEW[5]

The empirical literature on both international trade and foreign direct investment is vast, but the works that consider links between trade and foreign direct investment are much more limited. We will not review the well-known empirical trade literature here, but will review some of the published material on the determinants of FDI. This is especially important because it is often the motivation for FDI that determines its impact on trade. We then turn to studies that consider the link between FDI or foreign production and trade.

Determinants of FDI

There is a considerable body of literature on what determines where MNEs locate or expand their affiliates. The earliest studies cover questionnaire surveys in selected countries, with cross-sectional and time-series analysis of larger sets of data following on these. Much of the analysis is partial equilibrium in nature, but some general equilibrium studies have built on trade theory.

Caves (1996) and Dunning (1993) contain excellent reviews of the literature, some based on studies of the location decisions of outward FDI and some on inward FDI choices. One determinant of FDI that stands out in the earlier studies is barriers to trade. A positive relation with inward FDI also appears with size of GDP, per capita GDP, and the rate of growth of the local market. Distance variables are also related to inward FDI; for example, there is a positive relation to cultural similarity and transport costs. Production costs strongly influence FDI only in the case of export processing: wage rates, for example, do not receive much support as a determinant of inward FDI. The exchange rate is influential if the changes are long lived. Good innovating capacity tends to attract FDI. Natural resource availability is obviously important for FDI geared to exploiting this. Riskiness and political instability play a role also. More broadly, several policy variables — apart from general liberalization of policy on inward FDI — can also intervene in some circumstances. Fiscal incentives can have an impact, for example, in the case of investment choices in adjacent countries or regions, other things equal.

It is important to add that the signs on these variables are not always unambiguous, and the degree of significance varies in different tests. Ambiguity exists with regard to the effects of barriers to trade once firms are established abroad, for example. The influence of these and other variables can vary if breakouts are available for different types of investments or firms — between greenfields or takeover investments, final or intermediate goods trade, first-time investments or subsequent expansion, and so on. Finally, the determinants clearly overlap in some cases. One useful combination has been used by Dunning in various studies. He classifies inward FDI by distinguishing whether it seeks natural resources, markets, efficiency in terms of organizing and exploiting products or processes, and acquisition of various types of strategic assets. These four categories, of course, can also overlap.

It may help to give some specificity to the above by citing the work of Robert Grosse and his associates, which has influenced our own tests. Grosse and Trevino (1996) analyze in a gravity model framework the determinants of FDI flows into the United States from 23 countries on a bilateral basis over the period 1980–92. Their empirical results indicate that the main positive influences on inward FDI are home country exports to the United States and home country market size. The main negative influences are cultural differences between the home and the host (United States) countries, geographic distance, as well the exchange rate. Political risk, the cost of funds, relative rates of return and a Japan dummy were either insignificant or marginally significant. The analysis is also conducted using foreign production as the dependent variable. Although the R^2 statistic is much higher in the latter analysis, there were no significant differences between the two analyses. This result is important because it lends support to the notion that FDI may be a good proxy for foreign sales.

Grosse (1997) studies the determinants of aggregate FDI flows into several Latin American economies. Inflows of FDI were regressed on several country-specific determinants. Variables exhibiting a positive influence on FDI flows were GDP, per capita GDP, inflation, fiscal balance, and interest rates. Variables exhibiting a negative influence are official reserves, country risk, oil prices, and the growth rate of GDP. Only the coefficient estimate on the growth rate of GDP did not obtain the expected sign, and only inflation and official reserves were not statistically significant. It is interesting to point out that since GDP and total trade were highly correlated with FDI, the author retains the more important variable, namely GDP. That is, trade is dropped as a determinant of FDI.

The analysis in Grosse (1997) is extended to consider the link between inward FDI flows and capital formation. The model compares the growth of capital formation, less FDI, with the growth of FDI in Latin America. A positive correlation between these variables would indicate that FDI contributes to capital formation whereas a negative correlation would indicate it replaces domestic capital formation. The relationship is found to be positive and highly significant. Grosse interprets these results as indicating that FDI flows into Latin America indeed contribute to capital formation.

Links between trade and FDI

In this section, we review some of the more significant literature on this subject. Trade theory itself is ambiguous on the question of whether trade and factor mobility are substitutes. While the Heckscher-Ohlin theory regards trade and factor mobility as substitutes, subsequent developments in the theory have left the issue unresolved: everything depends upon the model being used. A recent survey of the historical experience from 1870 to 1940 rejects substitutability and leans toward complementarity. But this does not resolve the issue for recent experience (Collins O'Rourke and Williamson, 1997).

If we concentrate on FDI rather than on migration and capital flows more broadly defined, the results are still ambiguous, depending on the model, type of trade, and country experience. Much of the earlier Canadian literature on FDI assumed substitutability for manufactures: a substantial fraction of inward FDI was said to be induced by protection, for example. On the other hand, FDI in the natural resource sector was favourable to trade, both in terms of an inflow of goods financed by international investment and the eventual export of part of the resource.

With regard to manufactures, a review of some recent work illustrates the difficulty of providing a clear or single explanation of the links between trade and FDI. The articles in Globerman (1994) offer a good review of the issues involved. Graham (1994) probably contains the best statement of the issues of direct interest to the present paper. He suggests that the evidence points to modest support for the idea that FDI abroad makes a positive contribution to net exports and to the balance of payments. However, as Hufbauer and Adler (1968) demonstrated empirically in a classic study, the results depend heavily on how firms abroad respond in supplying the foreign market if home country's FDI doesn't occur; in addition, the results vary by regions. As Graham also notes, it is not clear if FDI abroad drives the increase in exports or whether both are responding to changes in the production process.

Pfaffermayr (1994) uses impulse response analysis and variance decompositions to examine the dynamic relationship between trade and FDI flows. Using aggregate quarterly data on Austrian FDI outflows and exports over the period 1960–91, the author finds a very slow dynamic response of both variables to an exogenous shock on the other. The analysis indicates the possibility of a positive effect of exogenously increased FDI on exports and a negative effect of exports on FDI. No significant long run effects are established.

Rao, Ahmad and Legault (1994) reinforce empirically the view that exports and outward Canadian FDI are complementary while also indicating that the latter had no significant effect on capital formation in Canada. These and other types of macro effects are critical to the sensitive issue of the effects of outward FDI on home employment. Gunderson and Verma (1994) explore this in detail, as well as the question of whether economic integration leads to harmonization of labour regulations. They conclude that these issues are largely unsettled, partly because of a lack of data. They and some of the other authors who contributed to the 1994 volume note that there is more agreement that outward FDI affects the composition of overall output in ways which could favour higher skill workers and prejudice those with lower skills. However, Blomstrom and Kokko (1994), in the same volume, express concern that the reverse may be happening with outward FDI from Sweden.

Rao, Ahmad and Barnes (1996), in analyzing trade and FDI patterns among APEC economies, observe that the growth of FDI has partly led and partly followed the growth in trade. Furthermore, the trends point to complementarity rather than substitutability between international trade and FDI within the APEC region. This is tested empirically by regressing total trade (exports plus imports) relative to GDP to the ratio of total FDI (inward plus outward) stock to GDP, an APEC dummy, and a time trend. The coefficient on the investment variable is positive and highly significant. This is interpreted as suggesting that there is a strong and complementary relationship between total trade and total FDI for the APEC region.

Most studies of the topic of this paper consider the link between trade and FDI flows or stocks. Brainard (1997) points out several problems with such studies. She argues that considering the link between exports and foreign direct investment is a conceptual mismatch, as the correct comparison is between exports and foreign production. Second, considering trade does not allow to distinguish between trade within multinationals and arms-length trade. There are studies however that are not subject to these criticisms.

Lipsey and Weiss (1981) use data for 1970 on exports from the United States and 13 other major countries to a cross-section of 44 countries. The exports are at the industry level. They use a gravity model with country size, distance, and membership in a trade bloc, and add to it some variables describing direct investment by the United States and other countries. The question being asked is whether direct investment has any impact on exports beyond the country characteristics. For the 14 industries studied, the level of U.S. affiliate activity is found to be positively related to U.S. exports to that country in the same industry, and negatively related to exports of rival producers. The presence of foreign countries' firms was negatively related to U.S. exports and positively related to foreign countries' exports. This is interpreted as indicating that U.S. manufacturing affiliate activity tends to promote U.S. exports and that foreign manufacturing affiliates tend to promote foreign country exports. As a result, there is no evidence that on balance, a country's production in overseas markets substitutes for its own domestic production and employment. Also, they find distance is insignificant in explaining exports when affiliate sales are included as a dependent variable.

Lipsey and Weiss (1984) use unpublished firm level data from the Bureau of Economic Analysis's 1970 survey and are able to improve on their 1981 study by disaggregating further by industry, location of investment and destination of exports. By comparing U.S.-owned production and trade across countries within industries, the authors avoid biases that may arise from the presence of industry comparative advantages that promote both trade and direct investment. Exports in 1970 to each of 5 areas of the world by individual firms are related to characteristics of the parent firm and to the output of overseas affiliates and the size of the market within each area. This is done within a gravity model framework. The results indicate that parent exports to an area (whether exports to non-affiliates are included or not) are almost always positively related to manufacturing affiliate activity in that area. That is, higher levels of affiliate output went along with higher exports by the parent. In general, at the industry level, higher foreign production increased parent exports of intermediate goods, while in final products there is either no effect or a positive one.

Horst (1972) uses data on U.S. affiliates in Canada and finds that affiliate production is increasing with tariffs, and both affiliate production and exports are increasing with R&D intensity. Swedenborg (1979) uses firm level data on Swedish multinationals. Multinational sales and exports are complements at the level of the firm. Proximity is not considered. Blomstrom et al. (1988) use industry level data on U.S. and Swedish multinationals and find that exports and foreign production are complementary. Proximity is excluded after it is found to be insignificant. Grubert and Mutti (1991) find that both exports and affiliate sales are increasing with distance, but neither is significantly affected by tariffs.

Perhaps the most thorough study on the links between exports and foreign production is Brainard (1997). The author controls for simultaneity between trade flows and multinational sales by using the share of total trade accounted for by multinational sales as the dependent variable, and by using instrumental variables to estimate the levels of multinational sales and trade. Furthermore, it is the first study to use a direct product-specific measure of transport costs as well as disaggregated data on tariffs; it also includes variables measuring concentration advantages. Brainard uses a gravity model to test the proximity-concentration hypothesis of MNE activity. She uses a 1989 cross-section of data on a bilateral basis between the United States and 27 other countries. The data are disaggregated at the 3-digit SIC industry level. These data come from the U.S. Bureau of Economic Analysis. The dependent variable is foreign production of MNEs, both abroad and in the United States. The gravity model used includes both aggregate and industry level variables. The aggregate measures are per capita GDP, corporate taxes, and measures of openness to trade and FDI. The industry level data are transport costs, tariffs, and scale economies. The scale economies are both at the plant and corporate levels. Also included in the gravity equation are dummy variables for political stability, adjacency, and an EC dummy. The results imply that overseas production increases relative to exports the higher the transport costs and trade barriers, and the lower the investment barriers and scale economies.

The proximity-concentration hypothesis tested by Brainard applies directly to the share of foreign production rather than the level. By using the share of foreign production as the dependent variable, the simultaneity problem between affiliate production and exports is avoided. In estimating the model in levels, the simultaneity problem is accounted for by using instrumental variables. Exports are instrumented with net exports, that is, all exports less those mediated by MNEs (exports to U.S.-owned affiliates and exports by foreign affiliates in the United States). A similar analysis is conducted on the inward side and similar results are obtained.

Summary

As discussed above, there is a conceptual problem involved in comparing exports to the FDI stock or even to FDI flows. The analogue to exports is foreign production or foreign sales. We would prefer to consider the link between Canadian exports and production by Canadian firms abroad on a bilateral-industry basis. Unfortunately, such data are not available for Canada. Such bilateral-industry level data does exist for U.S. multinational corporations. The benefit of using the U.S. data is, of course, that we solve this conceptual problem. The cost is that we can only analyze the behaviour of U.S. multinationals.

In this study, we are concerned with the behaviour of Canadian multinationals, and hence we are forced to use the FDI data. As a result, we use Canadian FDI stocks as a proxy for Canadian multinational production and sales abroad. Stocks are a better proxy for multinational production than are flows. It is also important to point out that bilateral FDI flow data are not available for Canada for many of the 35 countries. In Appendix C, we document that FDI stocks do proxy foreign sales quite well with respect to the United States.

We estimate a gravity model of Canada's trade with 35 countries. To this gravity model, we add measures of FDI stock. The test is therefore to see whether FDI has any predictive value for trade after determinants of international trade are accounted for. The gravity model has transaction costs as its source of comparative advantage. Our motivation for adding FDI stocks to the gravity model of trade is that the presence of such stocks may indicate a reduction of information and transaction costs between the two countries. Therefore, rather than simply serving as an alternative mode of servicing foreign markets, FDI may improve networks and hence cause increases in international trade. Our test, however, does not distinguish between these two views.

Literature review

Study	Title	Sample	Methodology	Conclusions
Grosse and Trevino (1996)	Foreign Direct Investment in the United States: An Analysis by Country of Origin *Journal of International Business Studies*	1980 to 1992	– Gravity model linking bilateral FDI into the United States from 23 countries to country specific determinants.	– Inward FDI is positively related to home country exports to the United States and to country size. – Negative influences on FDI are language differences, geographic differences, and exchange rates. – Political risk, cost of funds, relative rates of return and a Japan dummy are at best marginally significant.
Grosse (1997)	Foreign Direct Investment into Latin America Thunderbird Research Centre Discussion Paper	1980 to 1994	– Uses regression methodology to measure country specific determinants of aggregate FDI flows into Latin America.	– FDI inflows are positively related to GDP, GDP per capita, inflation, the fiscal balance and inflation. – Variables exhibiting a negative relationship are official reserves, country risk, oil prices and GDP growth. – The analysis is extended to show that FDI into Latin America contributes to domestic capital formation.
Jun and Singh (1996)	The Determinants of Foreign Direct Investment in Developing Countries *Transnational Corporations*	1970 to 1993	– Use regression methodology to analyze the determinants of aggregate FDI inflows into 31 developing countries.	– Find export orientation ranks among the strongest explanatory variables attracting FDI inflows. – This is interpreted as being consistent with the growing complementarity between trade and FDI.
Rao, Ahmad and Legault (1994)	Canadian-Based Multinationals: An Analysis of Activities and Performance *Canadian-Based Multinationals*			– The results reinforce empirically the view that exports and outward FDI are complementary. – There is no significant effect found of outward FDI on capital formation in Canada.

Literature review (cont'd)

Study	Title	Sample	Methodology	Conclusions
Rao, Ahmad and Barnes (1996)	Foreign Direct Investment and APEC Economic Integration Industry Canada Working Paper Series	1980 to 1995	– Use regression methodology to test links between trade and FDI within the APEC region. – Regress trade relative to GDP on total FDI relative to GDP, an APEC dummy and a time trend.	– Find that FDI has partly led and partly followed growth in trade, and is interpreted as a complementary relationship between trade and FDI within the APEC region. – That is, there is evidence of a strong and complementary relationship between total trade and total FDI within the APEC region.
Pfaffermayr (1994)	Foreign Direct Investment and Exports: A Time Series Approach *Applied Economics*	1960 to 1991	– Impulse response analysis and variance decompositions.	– Examines the dynamic relationship between Austrian trade and FDI flows. – Finds a very slow dynamic response of both variables to exogenous shocks to the other variable. – Interprets results as the possibility of a positive effect of exogenously increased FDI on exports, and a negative effect of exports on imports. – So significant long-run effects are established.
Lipsey and Weiss (1981)	Foreign Production and Exports in Manufacturing *Review of Economics and Statistics*	1970 data on exports to 44 countries from the United States and 13 other major countries	– Use a gravity model linking exports to country size, distance, and membership in a trade bloc. – Add to this variables measuring direct investment.	– For the 14 industries studied, the level of U.S. affiliate activity is found to be positively related to U.S. exports to that country and that industry, and negatively related to exports of rival producers. – The presence of foreign countries' firms was negatively related to U.S. exports and positively related to foreign countries' exports. – This indicates that U.S. manufacturing activity in foreign countries tends to promote U.S. exports. – No evidence of substitutability between own production and exports.

Literature review (cont'd)

Study	Title	Sample	Methodology	Conclusions
Lipsey and Weiss (1984)	Foreign Production and Exports of Individual Firms *Review of Economics and Statistics*	Use unpublished firm level data from 1970 BEA survey.	– Exports in 1970 to each of 5 areas of the world by individual firms are related to characteristics of the parent firm and to output of overseas affiliates and the size of the market within each area. – Done within a gravity model framework.	– Find that parent exports to an area (whether exports to non-affiliates are included or not) are almost always positively related to manufacturing affiliate activity in that area – In general, at the industry level, increased foreign production went along with higher exports of intermediate goods, while in final products there was either no effect or a positive one
Brainard (1997)	An Empirical Assessment of the Proximity-Concentration Trade-off between Multinational Sales and Trade *American Economic Review*	1989 cross-section of data on a bilateral basis between the United States and 27 other countries at the industry level.	– Uses a gravity model to test the links between MNE exports and foreign production. – Aggregate measures in the regression are per capita GDP, corporate taxes, openness to trade and FDI. – Industry measures are transport costs, tariffs and scale economies. – Also included are dummy variables for political stability, adjacency, and an EC dummy.	– The results imply that overseas production increases relative to exports. The higher the transport costs the higher the trade barriers. The lower the investment barriers the lower the scale economies.

3. DATA DESCRIPTION

In this paper, we consider empirical links between Canadian exports and outward FDI stocks, and Canadian imports and inward FDI stocks, on a bilateral basis for 35 countries. These data are on an annual basis and cover the period 1970–96. The trade and FDI data described in this section were obtained from CANSIM and Statistics Canada. Details are provided in Appendix B.

Table 1 contains data on the trade and FDI characteristics of the Canadian economy. It is readily apparent that both international trade and FDI are important to the Canadian economy. In 1970, merchandise exports and imports were 19 percent and 16 percent of GDP, respectively. These figures had increased dramatically to 36 percent and 30 percent in 1996. This is also reflected in the compound growth rates: over the 1970–96 period, exports and imports grew at real rates exceeding 5 percent, whereas GDP grew at 3.39 percent.

Turning to FDI, it is clear that there is an asymmetry in the trends related to outward and inward FDI stocks for Canada. In 1970, the ratio of outward FDI to GDP was 7 percent, whereas the ratio of inward FDI to GDP was 31 percent. The importance of inward FDI fell to 21 percent of GDP over the 1970s and has remained fairly constant at that ratio over the period 1980–96. In sharp contrast, the importance of outward FDI has increased dramatically to 22 percent of GDP in 1996. This is also reflected in the compound growth rates where outward FDI has grown at almost twice the rate of inward FDI over the 1970–96 period —13.4 percent and 7.5 percent, respectively. One qualification to these growth rates is that since FDI is reported at historical costs, we are not getting an accurate measure of growth rates. But what is clear, however, is that there is an increasing role being played by outward FDI in the economic integration of Canada to the world economy.

Converting data to real values

The data used in this study are expressed in real 1987 constant U.S. dollars. The GDP and GDP per capita data for the 35 foreign countries and Canada are available from the PENN world tables on that basis. These data have been constructed very carefully to allow for international comparisons (see Summers and Heston, 1991). Canadian exports and imports are available on a current Canadian dollar basis. These data were converted to a 1987 constant U.S. dollar basis.

Unlike exports and imports, it is a non-trivial task to convert the Canadian FDI stock figures from their present historical cost values to real values. We do not know of any attempts to undertake such a valuation for Canadian data. The difficulty with such a transformation arises because FDI is a stock. Consider the following equation:

$$\text{FDI}_t = \text{FDI}_{t-1} + \text{Retained earnings} + \textbf{Net flows of FDI} + \text{Price appreciation/depreciation on FDI}_{t-1}$$

The level of FDI at any point in time is defined as the level of FDI in the previous period, plus retained earnings, plus net new flows of FDI, plus price appreciation (or less depreciation). The retained earnings and the flows are in current dollars, and are simply added to the previous years FDI stock, which is not in current dollars. This is the balance of payments definition of FDI. However, there is another component that involves revaluation of the FDI stocks. It is this last component which is needed to convert FDI from historical costs to market values.

The United States Department of Commerce (1995) has published U.S. stock figures on the basis of historical costs, replacement costs, and market values, but the country and sectoral data are available only on a historical (book value) basis. There are a variety of private and semi-official estimates of the different valuations for the U.S. and U.K. stocks of FDI (Bellak and Cantwell, 1996). A straightforward way to adjust stock values is through changes in security prices, as utilized in Gray and Rugman (1994) but this is subject to a number of criticisms as noted in Bellak and Cantwell (1996). We have decided to use the unadjusted data.

Description of the aggregate data

We have obtained outward and inward FDI stocks, and exports and imports, on a bilateral basis between Canada and the 35 countries listed in Table 2.[6] The data cover the period 1970–96. Canada's trade and FDI relationship includes several countries in Europe (EC), East Asia (EA) and Latin America (LA). What is readily apparent, however, is the importance of high income countries: of the 35 countries listed, 19 are high income, 10 are middle income, and 3 are low income. Three countries (Bahamas, Bermuda, and the Netherlands Ant.) were not classified.

Table 3 gives the distribution of Canada's outward FDI stocks reported on a historical cost basis. The United States remains the primary location of Canada's outward FDI, with 54.38 percent of all Canadian outward FDI in 1996. This percentage was about the same as in 1970 (53.96 percent), but had increased to a peak of 69.5 percent in 1984, and decreased thereafter. In 1970, Brazil was the second largest location of Canadian outward FDI, at 9.94 percent, slightly more than the percentage for the United Kingdom in that year (9.75 percent). However, the United Kingdom was second by 1973, and has remained so thereafter. As with the United States, the percentage of Canadian outward FDI in the United Kingdom increased between 1970 and 1990, but has since fallen and is now back to what it was in 1970. We have seen a marked reduction in the percentage of Canadian FDI in Brazil, a less marked reduction for Australia, and an increase for Ireland. Overall, however, the percentage of Canadian outward FDI in the EC and East Asia has been increasing, but has been falling in Latin America. The percentage in APEC increased in the first part of the sample, but has been falling over the 1990s.

Table 4 gives the distribution of Canada's inward FDI stock. In 1970, 80.57 percent of all inward FDI in Canada had come from the United States. This ratio had fallen to 64.22 percent in 1990, but increased to 68.03 percent in 1996 with an upward trend beginning in 1993. The United Kingdom was the second largest source of FDI in Canada over the entire sample period, comprising from 8 to 13 percent of the total. The Netherlands, France, and Japan and, to a lesser extent, Hong Kong and Sweden have increased their share. The relative importance of Germany increased over the period 1970–90, but has decreased over the 1990s. Overall, the percentage of FDI coming from the EC and East Asia have been increasing, but it has fallen for APEC, and has remained about the same for Latin America.

Table 5 gives the distribution of Canada's exports to the 35 countries. In 1970 64.8 percent of Canadian exports went to the United States, a percentage that had decreased slightly in 1980 but had increased again to over 80 percent in 1996. The second largest recipient of Canada's exports in 1970, the United Kingdom saw its share fall steadily from 8.92 percent to only 1.46 percent in 1996, thus moving to third position. Japan was the third largest recipient of Canadian exports in 1970, and after some volatility was the second largest recipient of Canadian exports in 1996, at 4.04 percent. Germany has been the fourth largest recipient of Canada's exports over the entire sample, its share decreasing from 2.30 percent in 1970 to 1.21 percent in 1996. Overall, Canada's exports to APEC have increased over the sample period whereas exports to the EC have fallen.

Table 6 contains the distribution of Canada's imports. The percentage of imports coming from the United States has fallen steadily over the 1970s and 1980s, but it has increased over the 1990s. There has been a steady increase in the importance of Mexico, Ireland, Singapore and Indonesia. Overall, however, no region has experience a steady increase or decrease in relative importance over the sample period.

We note in Table 7 that the share of Canada's outward FDI to the top five recipients has fallen since 1980 while the share of Canada's exports has increased. On the inward side, by contrast, the share of FDI accounted for by the top 5 source countries has fallen. This is true for imports as well.

Summary

These data demonstrate the increasing role played by both outward and inward FDI in the integration of the Canadian economy with both the European Community and East Asia. In contrast, the importance of these regions in terms of exports and imports has fallen or has not increased dramatically. The importance of APEC as a source of FDI has decreased, whereas it has increased as a destination for Canadian outward FDI. On the other hand, the importance of APEC as a destination for Canadian exports has increased steadily, whereas the importance of Canada as a destination for APEC exports has been quite stable. There is very little FDI in Canada that originates in Latin America, but that region hosts 2 to 3 percent of Canadian outward FDI. Also, Canada imports 2 to 3 times more from Latin America than it exports to the region. There does not seem to be any significant trend in the Latin American data vis a vis Canada, with the exception of course of the dramatic reduction in importance of Brazil as a destination for Canadian FDI.

Description of the industry level data

The trade data are available at the industry level according to the traditional SIC-E (establishment) classification. The FDI data, however, are available at the SIC-C (company) classification. The SIC-C classification involves re-aligning the 4-digit SIC-E classification to produce a new classification defined specifically to take into account the integrated operations of complex businesses. While in the SIC-E only specialized classes exist, the SIC-C contains both specialized classes and classes for business with combined activities.

These SIC-E trade data were transformed by the authors to accord with the SIC-C classification. We have therefore compiled Canadian trade and FDI data at the industry level which are directly comparable. These data include outward FDI and exports at the industry level to all countries (Table 8), to the United States (Table 9), and to the United Kingdom (Table 10). On the inward side, we have inward FDI and imports from all countries (Table 11), from the United States (Table 12), from the United Kingdom (Table 13), and from Japan (Table 14). These data cover the period 1983–95.[7]

Table 8a gives the distribution of Canada's outward FDI stock to the world at the industry level. In 1995, almost one quarter of all outward Canadian FDI was in finance and insurance, followed by metallic minerals and metals products with 16.22 percent, and energy with 8.54 percent. Trends in these data over the 1983 to 1995 period include dramatic reductions in the relative importance of energy, whose share has fallen by half over the period. The finance and insurance sector has seen its share more than double. Other industries of growth are communications; accommodations, restaurants, recreation services and food retailing; and to a lesser extend transportation equipment and electrical and electronic products. Industries that are falling in importance are food, beverage and tobacco; energy; chemicals, chemical products and textiles; and construction and related activities. Wood and paper; machinery and equipment; and consumer goods and services remained relatively unchanged.

Table 8b gives the distribution of Canada's exports to the world at the industry level. What is immediately striking about the relative importance of Canada's exports at the industry level is its stability. Transportation equipment; wood and paper; and energy remain Canada's most important sources of exports, followed by metallic minerals and metal products; chemicals, chemical products and textiles; electrical and electronic products; and food beverage and tobacco. Machinery and equipment; and consumer goods and services are relatively less important sectors.

Table 9 depicts Canada's FDI and export relationships with the United States. Canadian FDI has fallen dramatically in construction and related activities; energy; and chemicals, chemical products and textiles. These have been offset by increases in communications; finance and insurance; and accommodations, restaurants, recreation services; and food retailing; and to a lesser extent in transportation equipment. Canadian exports to the United States are predominantly in transportation equipment, which accounted for one third of Canadian exports to the United States. Also important are wood and paper and energy.

Table 10 describes Canada's trade and FDI position with the United Kingdom. There have been dramatic changes in this bilateral relationship. In 1995, the share of Canadian FDI in food, beverage and tobacco had fallen to one third of its value in 1983. The share of metallic minerals and metal products had fallen to less than half of its1983 value. Construction and related activities went from nearly 10 percent in 1983 to less than 1 percent in 1995. These have been offset by dramatic growth in communications and in electrical and electronic products, and less dramatic growth in energy and in transportation equipment. As for Canadian exports to the United Kingdom, the dominant industries are wood and paper, metallic minerals and metal products, and energy.

Table 11 describes Canada's inward FDI and imports from the world. Finance and Insurance is the largest industry for inward FDI, followed by energy; chemicals, chemical products and textiles; transportation equipment; and food beverage and tobacco. Finance and insurance; electrical and electronic products; and food beverage and tobacco have seen increases in their relative importance, whereas energy, has seen a large reduction. Other industries have been relatively stable. As with Canada's exports to the world, Canada's imports from the world are also quite stable across industries. The most important imports for Canada remain transportation equipment; electrical and electronic products; chemicals, chemical products and textiles; and metallic minerals and metal products.

Table 12 describes Canada's imports and inward FDI from the United States. The largest change in U.S. FDI in Canada has been the reduction in importance of the energy sector. The most important industry for U.S. FDI in Canada is finance and insurance, followed closely by transportation equipment; chemicals, chemical products and textiles; and energy. The most important Canadian imports from the United States remain transportation equipment, followed by chemicals, chemical products and textiles, electrical and electronic products, and machinery and equipment.

Table 13 describes Canada's imports and inward FDI from the United Kingdom. One third of U.K. FDI in Canada is in finance and insurance, followed by food, beverage and tobacco. These are also the only two industries that have seen any significant growth in their shares. Industries that have seen significant reductions in their shares are consumer goods and services, and energy. Canada's most important imports from the United Kingdom are energy, followed by chemicals, chemical products and textiles, machinery and equipment, and electrical and electronic products. Consumer goods and services and food, beverage and tobacco have seen large reductions in their relative importance.

Table 14 describes Canada's imports and inward FDI from Japan. The most important industry for Japanese FDI in Canada is transportation equipment, followed closely by wood and paper, metallic minerals and metal products, and finance and insurance. Imports from Japan are concentrated in 3 industries: electrical and electronic products, transportation equipment, and machinery and equipment.

Tables 15 to 18 revisit inward FDI and imports, but rather than using the industrial distribution of FDI as in the previous tables, we consider the distribution of the importance of source countries for both inward FDI and imports by sector and by year. The United States is the major foreign player in all Canadian industries in every year, by a considerable margin in each case. For example, in 1995, of all FDI in Canadian transportation services and communications, 87 percent originated in the United States. The United States played its smallest role in finance and insurance, but still held over 50 percent of all FDI in that industry. In terms of imports, the United States has shares of over 50 percent in all but two industries: energy, and consumer goods and services.

The United Kingdom held 21 percent of FDI in food, beverage and tobacco, 18 percent in finance and insurance, and 10 percent in construction and related activities. In terms of imports, the United Kingdom had the largest share of total Canadian imports in energy, with less than 3 percent in most other industries. The only industry in which Japan holds more than 10 percent of FDI is wood and paper. Japan's largest share in imports was in electrical and electronic products, followed by machinery and equipment, and transportation equipment.

Table 18 considers the relative importance of all counties other than the United States, United Kingdom and Japan. If one adds these three countries, at least 70 percent of the overall distribution of every sector is covered in every year, with a few exceptions; indeed, in most cases the top three countries account for at least 80 percent of the total. In 1995, only the energy sector received more than 30 percent of its FDI from countries other than the United States, United Kingdom and Japan, and only finance and insurance, and metallic minerals and metal products received more than 20 percent. These numbers are in sharp contrast to those for imports, where the relative importance of other countries is far more important.

Table 1
Trade and FDI characteristics of the Canadian economy
(millions of Canadian dollars / percentage)

	1970	1980	1990	1996
GDP ($)	87,312	303,954	675,852	771,470
Exports ($)	16,802	76,159	148,979	275,921
Imports ($)	13,952	69,274	136,224	233,114
(ratio)	(1.20)	(1.10)	(1.09)	(1.18)
Outward FDI stock ($)	6,520	28,413	98,402	170,845
Inward FDI stock ($)	27,374	64,708	130,932	180,394
(ratio)	(0.24)	(0.44)	(0.75)	(0.95)
Exports / GDP (percent)	0.19	0.25	0.22	0.36
Imports / GDP (percent)	0.16	0.23	0.20	0.30
Outward FDI stock / GDP (percent)	0.07	0.09	0.15	0.22
Inward FDI stock / GDP (percent)	0.31	0.21	0.19	0.23

Compound growth rates, nominal (real)

	1970–80	1980–90	1990–96	1970–96
GDP ($)	13.3	8.3	2.2	8.7
(real)	(4.64)	(2.97)	(2.03)	(3.39)
Exports ($)	16.3	6.9	10.8	11.4
(real)	(4.63)	(5.50)	(5.35)	(5.13)
Imports ($)	17.4	7.0	9.4	11.4
(real)	(7.28)	(5.45)	(4.54)	(5.94)
Outward FDI stock ($)	15.9	13.2	9.6	13.4
Inward FDI stock ($)	9.0	7.3	5.5	7.5

Table 2
Countries included in the study

Country	GNP per capita*	EC	East Asia	APEC	Latin America
1 United States	H			X	
2 Bahamas					
3 Bermuda					
4 Netherlands Ant.					
5 Mexico	M			X	X
6 Brazil	M				X
7 Venezuela	M				X
8 Panama	L				X
9 United Kingdom	H	X			
10 Ireland	H	X			
11 Netherlands	H	X			
12 Germany	H	X			
13 Switzerland	H				
14 France	H	X			
15 Belgium-Luxembourg	H	X			
16 Greece	M	X			
17 Spain	H	X			
18 Italy	H	X			
19 Portugal	M	X			
20 Austria	H				
21 Denmark	H	X			
22 Norway	H				
23 Sweden	H				
24 South Africa	M				
25 Singapore	H		X	X	
26 Australia	H			X	
27 Indonesia	L		X	X	
28 Hong Kong	H		X	X	
29 Japan	H		X	X	
30 Taiwan	M		X	X	
31 Malaysia	M		X	X	
32 South Korea	M		X	X	
33 India	L				
34 Saudi Arabia	M				
35 Israel	H				

* Indicates whether the country is a high (H), medium (M), or low (L) income country as classified in the World Bank's *World Development Report*. Not included in the World Bank's list are The Bahamas, Bermuda, and The Netherlands Ant.

Table 3
Distribution of Canada's outward FDI stock (percentage)

Country	1970	1980	1990	1996
0 All countries	100.00	100.00	100.00	100.00
1 United States	53.96	62.82	61.02	54.38
2 Bahamas	2.87	1.50	1.98	1.40
3 Bermuda	2.09	3.53	1.79	2.00
4 Netherlands Ant.	0.09	0.54	0.07	0.40
5 Mexico	0.69	0.58	0.25	0.74
6 Brazil	9.94	2.43	1.73	1.61
7 Venezuela	0.18	0.21	0.05	0.21
8 Panama	0.03	0.05	0.02	0.06
9 United Kingdom	9.75	10.84	9.78	9.78
10 Ireland	0.66	0.82	1.29	3.53
11 Netherlands	0.80	1.06	1.51	1.12
12 Germany	1.18	0.97	0.91	1.53
13 Switzerland	0.32	1.02	1.28	0.71
14 France	1.26	1.02	1.77	1.62
15 Belgium-Luxembourg	0.61	0.26	0.56	1.83
16 Greece	0.02	0.11	0.09	0.06
17 Spain	0.52	0.59	0.53	0.09
18 Italy	0.81	0.44	0.39	0.41
19 Portugal	0.02	0.04	0.12	0.06
20 Austria	0.15	0.11	0.01	0.12
21 Denmark	0.05	0.28	0.05	0.02
22 Norway	1.04	0.23	0.06	0.01
23 Sweden	0.03	0.04	0.03	0.14
24 South Africa	1.12	0.56	0.02	0.09
25 Singapore	0.03	0.03	1.87	1.40
26 Australia	3.63	2.44	2.44	1.93
27 Indonesia	0.37	2.08	0.95	0.83
28 Hong Kong	0.00	0.14	0.68	1.37
29 Japan	0.74	0.38	0.93	1.59
30 Taiwan	0.00	0.06	0.16	0.10
31 Malaysia	0.03	0.07	0.08	0.07
32 South Korea	0.00	0.00	0.02	0.08
33 India	0.52	0.21	0.10	0.11
34 Saudi Arabia	n.a.	n.a.	n.a.	n.a.
35 Israel	n.a.	n.a.	n.a.	n.a.
Total of listed countries	93.51	95.46	96.51	89.40
Regional distribution				
European Community	15.68	16.43	20.97	20.05
East Asia	1.17	2.76	4.69	5.44
APEC (less United States)	5.49	5.78	7.38	8.11
United States	53.96	62.82	61.02	54.38
Latin America	10.84	3.27	2.05	2.62

Table 4
Distribution of Canada's inward FDI stock (percentage)

Country	1970	1980	1990	1996
0 All countries	100.00	100.00	100.00	100.00
1 United States	80.57	77.84	64.22	68.03
2 Bahamas	0.27	0.20	0.11	0.07
3 Bermuda	0.11	1.02	0.99	0.87
4 Netherlands Ant.	0.04	0.08	0.07	0.10
5 Mexico	0.02	0.00	0.01	0.13
6 Brazil	n.a.	n.a.	n.a.	n.a.
7 Venezuela	0.01	0.00	0.00	0.00
8 Panama	0.06	0.15	0.09	0.05
9 United Kingdom	9.65	8.92	13.13	7.85
10 Ireland	0.02	0.13	0.06	0.05
11 Netherlands	1.65	1.88	3.27	4.07
12 Germany	1.33	2.79	3.88	3.03
13 Switzerland	1.29	1.48	2.21	2.11
14 France	1.74	1.99	2.93	3.18
15 Belgium-Luxembourg	0.95	1.05	0.51	1.81
16 Greece	0.00	0.00	0.01	0.01
17 Spain	0.00	0.03	0.03	0.01
18 Italy	0.25	0.10	0.25	0.17
19 Portugal	n.a.	n.a.	n.a.	n.a.
20 Austria	0.01	0.03	0.19	0.05
21 Denmark	0.05	0.05	0.01	0.11
22 Norway	0.02	0.03	0.46	0.31
23 Sweden	0.46	0.50	0.48	0.61
24 South Africa	n.a.	n.a.	n.a.	n.a.
25 Singapore	0.00	0.00	0.07	0.18
26 Australia	0.04	0.11	0.58	0.19
27 Indonesia	n.a.	n.a.	n.a.	n.a.
28 Hong Kong	0.07	0.08	1.05	1.67
29 Japan	0.38	0.93	3.99	3.59
30 Taiwan	0.00	0.00	0.01	0.08
31 Malaysia	0.00	0.00	0.02	0.02
32 South Korea	0.00	0.00	0.24	0.10
33 India	0.02	0.00	0.01	0.00
34 Saudi Arabia	0.00	0.02	0.05	0.02
35 Israel	0.00	0.00	0.07	0.06
Total of listed countries	99.01	99.41	99.00	98.53
Regional distribution				
European Community	15.64	16.94	24.08	20.29
East Asia	0.45	1.01	5.38	5.64
APEC (less United States)	0.51	1.12	5.97	5.96
United States	80.57	77.84	64.22	68.03
Latin America	0.09	0.15	0.10	0.18

Table 5
Distribution of Canada's exports (percentage)

Country	1970	1980	1990	1996
0 All countries	100.00	100.00	100.00	100.00
1 United States	64.80	63.25	74.88	80.99
2 Bahamas	0.10	0.03	0.03	0.01
3 Bermuda	0.07	0.04	0.02	0.01
4 Netherlands Ant.	0.03	0.01	0.01	0.01
5 Mexico	0.57	0.65	0.44	0.45
6 Brazil	0.55	1.26	0.34	0.52
7 Venezuela	0.67	0.89	0.19	0.23
8 Panama	0.05	0.07	0.01	0.02
9 United Kingdom	8.92	4.26	2.38	1.46
10 Ireland	0.09	0.15	0.09	0.09
11 Netherlands	1.67	1.89	1.11	0.60
12 Germany	2.30	2.19	1.56	1.21
13 Switzerland	0.25	0.51	0.71	0.34
14 France	0.93	1.34	0.88	0.63
15 Belgium-Luxembourg	1.14	1.32	0.84	0.56
16 Greece	0.14	0.17	0.07	0.04
17 Spain	0.40	0.31	0.26	0.19
18 Italy	1.11	1.32	0.80	0.49
19 Portugal	0.07	0.13	0.12	0.04
20 Austria	0.05	0.10	0.11	0.15
21 Denmark	0.13	0.12	0.09	0.04
22 Norway	1.06	0.46	0.37	0.31
23 Sweden	0.29	0.38	0.22	0.10
24 South Africa	0.63	0.27	0.12	0.08
25 Singapore	0.07	0.26	0.27	0.21
26 Australia	1.20	0.89	0.61	0.37
27 Indonesia	0.10	0.28	0.21	0.34
28 Hong Kong	0.13	0.26	0.46	0.44
29 Japan	4.83	5.74	5.52	4.04
30 Taiwan	0.11	0.33	0.54	0.51
31 Malaysia	0.09	0.13	0.17	0.19
32 South Korea	0.11	0.67	1.04	1.02
33 India	0.78	0.47	0.22	0.13
34 Saudi Arabia	0.04	0.41	0.19	0.23
35 Israel	0.09	0.15	0.10	0.09
Total of listed countries	93.57	90.71	94.98	96.14
Regional distribution				
European Community	16.90	13.20	8.20	5.35
East Asia	5.44	7.67	8.21	6.75
APEC (less United States)	7.21	9.21	9.26	7.57
United States	64.80	63.25	74.88	80.99
Latin America	1.84	2.87	0.98	1.22

Table 6
Distribution of Canada's imports (percentage)

Country	1970	1980	1990	1996
0 All countries	100.00	100.00	100.00	100.00
1 United States	71.10	69.30	64.50	67.60
2 Bahamas	0.05	0.05	0.02	0.01
3 Bermuda	0.00	0.00	0.00	0.00
4 Netherlands Ant.	0.39	0.11	0.01	0.01
5 Mexico	0.34	0.50	1.28	2.59
6 Brazil	0.35	0.51	0.59	0.49
7 Venezuela	2.43	3.20	0.42	0.31
8 Panama	0.05	0.06	0.00	0.01
9 United Kingdom	5.29	2.85	3.55	2.53
10 Ireland	0.09	0.15	0.19	0.25
11 Netherlands	0.57	0.36	0.53	0.40
12 Germany	2.66	2.13	2.82	2.07
13 Switzerland	0.58	0.73	0.48	0.40
14 France	1.14	1.14	1.80	1.46
15 Belgium-Luxembourg	0.37	0.35	0.42	0.37
16 Greece	0.04	0.04	0.05	0.03
17 Spain	0.25	0.28	0.36	0.29
18 Italy	1.04	0.90	1.44	1.17
19 Portugal	0.10	0.08	0.13	0.08
20 Austria	0.33	0.15	0.30	0.26
21 Denmark	0.22	0.17	0.18	0.15
22 Norway	0.35	0.12	1.24	1.19
23 Sweden	0.76	0.61	0.66	0.52
24 South Africa	0.33	0.54	0.10	0.19
25 Singapore	0.14	0.18	0.41	0.51
26 Australia	1.05	0.75	0.56	0.55
27 Indonesia	0.00	0.08	0.15	0.27
28 Hong Kong	0.56	0.82	0.78	0.49
29 Japan	4.17	4.11	6.99	4.48
30 Taiwan	0.37	0.82	1.55	1.23
31 Malaysia	0.24	0.18	0.28	0.68
32 South Korea	0.10	0.61	1.65	1.17
33 India	0.29	0.14	0.17	0.26
34 Saudi Arabia	0.17	3.68	0.52	0.28
35 Israel	0.10	0.08	0.09	0.11
Total of listed countries	96.02	95.78	94.22	92.41
Regional distribution				
European Community	11.77	8.45	11.47	8.80
East Asia	5.58	6.80	11.81	8.83
APEC (less United States)	6.97	8.05	13.65	11.97
United States	71.10	69.30	64.50	67.60
Latin America	3.17	4.27	2.29	3.40

Table 7
Concentration of Canada's FDI and trade

	1970	1980	1990	1996
Percent of outward FDI accounted for by top recipients:				
1	53.96	62.82	61.02	54.38
2	63.90	73.66	74.77	64.16
3	73.65	77.19	77.21	67.69
4	77.28	79.63	79.19	69.69
5	80.15	82.06	80.98	71.62
Percent of inward FDI accounted for by top sources:				
1	80.57	77.84	64.22	68.03
2	90.22	86.76	77.35	75.88
3	91.96	89.55	81.34	79.95
4	93.61	91.54	85.22	83.54
5	94.94	93.42	88.49	86.72
Percent of exports accounted for by top recipients:				
1	64.80	63.25	74.88	80.99
2	73.72	68.99	80.40	85.03
3	78.55	73.25	82.78	86.49
4	80.85	75.44	84.34	87.70
5	85.52	77.33	85.45	88.72
Percent of imports accounted for by top sources:				
1	71.10	69.30	64.50	67.60
2	76.39	73.41	71.49	72.08
3	80.56	77.09	75.04	74.67
4	83.22	80.29	77.86	77.20
5	85.65	83.14	79.66	79.27

Table 8a
Industrial distribution of Canada's outward FDI stock in all countries (percentage)

Industries (SIC-C 1980)	1983	1987	1990	1995
1. Food, Beverage and Tobacco	9.01	7.55	8.31	6.75
2. Wood and Paper	3.69	3.95	3.84	3.35
3. Energy	16.63	8.75	7.70	8.54
4. Chemicals, Chemical Products and Textiles	8.85	7.70	7.60	4.67
5. Metallic Minerals and Metal Products	18.97	15.93	14.38	16.22
6. Machinery and Equipment	0.44	0.71	1.20	0.81
7. Transportation Equipment	1.50	2.09	2.32	2.72
8. Electrical and Electronic Products	3.56	4.70	5.48	5.93
9. Construction and Related Activities	12.57	7.90	7.48	3.28
10. Transportation Services	3.28	4.18	4.97	3.47
11. Communications	5.85	7.17	8.21	10.00
12. Finance and Insurance	10.79	21.24	23.80	23.67
13. Accommodation, Restaurants, Recreation Services and Food Retailing	1.23	2.22	2.02	6.23
14. Consumer Goods and Services	3.26	5.17	1.50	3.44
15. Other	0.38	0.74	1.18	0.92
Total	100.00	100.00	100.00	100.00

Table 8b
Industrial distribution of Canada's exports to all countries (percentage)

Industries (SIC-C 1980)	1983	1987	1990	1995
1. Food, Beverage and Tobacco	13.21	10.02	9.47	8.27
2. Wood and Paper	15.15	17.72	15.95	16.73
3. Energy	16.57	11.88	13.32	11.30
4. Chemicals, Chemical Products and Textiles	7.49	8.18	7.75	8.74
5. Metallic Minerals and Metal Products	8.25	8.00	10.32	9.50
6. Machinery and Equipment	4.77	4.76	4.80	5.35
7. Transportation Equipment	27.76	30.77	28.29	28.10
8. Electrical and Electronic Products	4.48	5.72	7.17	8.35
9. Construction and Related Activities	0.90	0.84	0.76	0.67
10. Transportation Services	0.00	0.00	0.00	0.00
11. Communications	0.39	0.57	0.40	0.51
12. Finance and Insurance	0.00	0.00	0.00	0.00
13. Accommodation, Restaurants, Recreation Services and Food Retailing	0.00	0.02	0.04	0.04
14. Consumer Goods and Services	1.02	1.52	1.72	2.43
15. Other	0.00	0.00	0.02	0.01
Total	100.00	100.00	100.0	100.00

Table 9a
Industrial distribution of Canada's outward FDI stock in the United States (percentage)

Industries (SIC-C 1980)	1983	1987	1990	1995
1. Food, Beverage and Tobacco	8.59	6.78	8.09	5.76
2. Wood and Paper	4.76	3.96	3.99	4.42
3. Energy	17.79	8.23	8.55	7.71
4. Chemicals, Chemical Products and Textiles	11.76	10.43	10.89	3.84
5. Metallic Minerals and Metal Products	13.05	14.34	12.88	15.24
6. Machinery and Equipment	0.18	0.49	0.87	0.64
7 Transportation Equipment	0.37	1.68	1.52	2.18
8. Electrical and Electronic Products	4.85	5.36	6.93	5.26
9. Construction and Related Activities	17.17	11.45	8.30	4.93
10. Transportation Services	2.27	5.78	6.81	5.17
11. Communications	7.25	8.21	10.24	10.92
12. Finance and Insurance	6.11	12.86	16.80	16.02
13. Accommodation, Restaurants, Recreation Services and Food Retailing	1.82	3.27	2.44	11.15
14. Consumer Goods and Services	3.54	6.39	0.83	5.95
15. Other	0.49	0.76	0.85	0.81
Total	100.00	100.00	100.00	100.00

Table 9b
Industrial distribution of Canada's exports to the United States (percentage)

Industries SIC-C 1980)	1983	1987	1990	1995
1. Food, Beverage and Tobacco	4.96	5.28	5.49	5.21
2. Wood and Paper	14.95	16.23	14.66	14.20
3. Energy	19.68	12.89	13.60	12.17
4. Chemicals, Chemical Products and Textiles	6.18	6.44	7.28	8.72
5. Metallic Minerals and Metal Products	7.08	6.91	7.66	8.62
6. Machinery and Equipment	4.84	4.86	4.84	5.39
7. Transportation Equipment	35.91	38.69	35.86	33.13
8. Electrical and Electronic Products	4.30	5.70	7.66	8.67
9. Construction and Related Activities	0.57	0.70	0.54	0.56
10. Transportation Services	0.00	0.00	0.00	0.00
11. Communications	0.49	0.68	0.47	0.57
12. Finance and Insurance	0.00	0.00	0.00	0.00
13. Accommodation, Restaurants, Recreation Services and Food Retailing	0.00	0.03	0.04	0.04
14. Consumer Goods and Services	1.06	1.60	1.89	2.71
15. Other	0.00	0.00	0.02	0.01
Total	100.00	100.0	100.00	100.00

Table 10a
Industrial distribution of Canada's outward FDI stock in the United Kingdom (percentage)

Industries (SIC-C 1980)	1983	1987	1990	1995
1. Food, Beverage and Tobacco	28.32	20.41	9.56	9.00
2. Wood and Paper	2.47	10.29	5.29	2.16
3. Energy	8.51	8.74	7.39	11.69
4. Chemicals, Chemical Products and Textiles	1.12	1.28	0.44	0.64
5. Metallic Minerals and Metal Products	24.66	15.57	9.48	11.52
6. Machinery and Equipment	1.35	3.15	2.44	1.04
7. Transportation Equipment	0.00	1.00	2.92	3.11
8. Electrical and Electronic Products	1.80	8.14	6.11	13.02
9. Construction and Related Activities	8.57	2.25	17.51	0.91
10. Transportation Services	1.93	0.76	1.32	0.33
11. Communications	2.95	7.90	6.90	29.61
12. Finance and Insurance	13.39	17.37	22.24	11.85
13. Accommodation, Restaurants, Recreation Services and Food Retailing	0.00	0.82	3.90	0.94
14. Consumer Goods and Services	4.14	0.98	0.35	1.11
15. Other	0.77	1.34	4.15	3.07
Total	100.00	100.00	100.00	100.00

Table 10b
Industrial distribution of Canada's exports to the United Kingdom (percentage)

Industries (SIC-C 1980)	1983	1987	1990	1995
1. Food, Beverage and Tobacco	21.78	11.98	10.05	8.99
2. Wood and Paper	28.59	34.06	31.97	23.96
3. Energy	5.18	6.25	10.11	12.34
4. Chemicals, Chemical Products and Textiles	8.12	7.46	5.86	5.46
5. Metallic Minerals and Metal Products	21.12	19.71	19.81	19.86
6. Machinery and Equipment	3.80	4.16	5.23	5.11
7. Transportation Equipment	3.18	6.26	6.53	4.42
8. Electrical and Electronic Products	5.54	7.70	7.46	16.19
9. Construction and Related Activities	1.11	0.49	0.56	0.40
10. Transportation Services	0.00	0.00	0.00	0.00
11. Communications	0.24	0.34	0.45	0.60
12. Finance and Insurance	0.00	0.00	0.00	0.00
13. Accommodation, Restaurants, Recreation Services and Food Retailing	0.00	0.00	0.11	0.05
14. Consumer Goods and Services	1.33	1.58	1.77	2.58
15. Other	0.00	0.00	0.10	0.04
Total	100.00	100.00	100.00	100.00

Table 11a
Industrial distribution of Canada's inward FDI stock from all countries (percentage)

Industries (SIC-C 1980)	1983	1987	1990	1995
1. Food, Beverage and Tobacco	5.66	7.03	7.03	9.49
2. Wood and Paper	4.09	4.99	5.81	4.70
3. Energy	25.86	19.48	16.42	11.68
4. Chemicals, Chemical Products and Textiles	11.20	8.55	10.36	10.90
5. Metallic Minerals and Metal Products	6.34	5.51	7.44	6.07
6. Machinery and Equipment	3.76	4.05	3.98	4.20
7. Transportation Equipment	8.58	12.00	10.02	10.72
8. Electrical and Electronic Products	3.99	6.28	5.56	7.10
9. Construction and Related Activities	5.46	6.10	5.36	6.49
10+11. Transportation Services and Communications	1.61	1.82	2.47	3.02
12. Finance and Insurance	13.27	16.99	18.87	18.04
13. Accommodation, Restaurants, Recreation Services and Food Retailing	n.a.	n.a.	n.a.	n.a.
14. Consumer Goods and Services	6.92	4.12	3.86	4.64
15. Other	3.26	3.06	2.83	2.95
Total	100.00	100.00	100.00	100.00

Table 11b
Industrial distribution of Canada's imports from all countries (percentage)

Industries (SIC-C 1980)	1983	1987	1990	1995
1. Food, Beverage and Tobacco	7.72	6.75	6.74	6.21
2. Wood and Paper	2.64	2.56	2.74	2.94
3. Energy	8.01	5.59	6.74	4.04
4. Chemicals, Chemical Products and Textiles	11.84	11.04	11.95	13.58
5. Metallic Minerals and Metal Products	7.63	7.32	8.05	8.39
6. Machinery and Equipment	13.03	13.66	13.52	12.91
7. Transportation Equipment	30.43	33.40	27.18	26.84
8. Electrical and Electronic Products	11.01	11.75	14.32	17.30
9. Construction and Related Activities	0.61	0.75	0.81	0.65
10. Transportation Services	0.00	0.00	0.00	0.00
11. Communications	1.67	1.31	1.59	1.45
12. Finance and Insurance	0.00	0.00	0.00	0.00
13. Accommodation, Restaurants, Recreation Services and Food Retailing	0.01	0.01	0.07	0.05
14. Consumer Goods and Services	5.39	5.86	6.26	5.62
15. Other	0.00	0.00	0.04	0.01
Total	100.00	100.00	100.00	100.00

Table 12a
Industrial distribution of Canada's inward FDI stock from the United States (percentage)

Industries (SIC-C 1980)	1983	1987	1990	1995
1. Food, Beverage and Tobacco	5.83	7.31	6.64	8.31
2. Wood and Paper	3.75	3.31	6.51	5.15
3. Energy	26.07	19.99	16.73	9.85
4. Chemicals, Chemical Products and Textiles	12.22	9.61	10.50	11.62
5. Metallic Minerals and Metal Products	7.18	5.77	6.23	5.86
6. Machinery and Equipment	4.69	4.71	4.74	4.84
7. Transportation Equipment	9.88	14.46	12.52	13.49
8. Electrical and Electronic Products	4.53	7.62	7.19	8.74
9. Construction and Related Activities	2.56	4.96	4.79	6.79
10+11. Transportation Services and Communications	1.83	2.24	3.10	3.93
12. Finance and Insurance	11.45	12.46	14.05	13.88
13. Accommodation, Restaurants, Recreation Services and Food Retailing	n.a.	n.a.	n.a.	n.a.
14. Consumer Goods and Services	6.21	4.21	4.19	5.15
15. Other	3.79	3.34	2.80	2.40
Total	100.00	100.00	100.00	100.00

Table 12b
Industrial distribution of Canada's imports from the United States (percentage)

Industries (SIC-C 1980)	1983	1987	1990	1995
1. Food, Beverage and Tobacco	6.17	5.37	5.82	5.43
2. Wood and Paper	2.98	2.92	3.43	3.84
3. Energy	4.58	3.18	3.08	1.49
4. Chemicals, Chemical Products and Textiles	11.77	10.72	12.76	14.47
5. Metallic Minerals and Metal Products	7.11	6.68	8.40	8.24
6. Machinery and Equipment	14.20	13.35	14.27	13.18
7. Transportation Equipment	37.18	41.41	32.32	33.09
8. Electrical and Electronic Products	10.97	11.84	14.06	14.40
9. Construction and Related Activities	0.57	0.71	0.83	0.59
10. Transportation Services	0.00	0.00	0.00	0.00
11. Communications	2.07	1.66	2.05	1.86
12. Finance and Insurance	0.00	0.00	0.00	0.00
13. Accommodation, Restaurants, Recreation Services and Food Retailing	0.02	0.01	0.08	0.06
14. Consumer Goods and Services	2.39	2.14	2.87	3.34
15. Other	0.00	0.00	0.03	0.01
Total	100.00	100.00	100.00	100.00

Table 13a
Industrial distribution of Canada's inward FDI stock from the United Kingdom (percentage)

Industries (SIC-C 1980)	1983	1987	1990	1995
1. Food, Beverage and Tobacco	9.13	12.68	17.16	20.70
2. Wood and Paper	4.74	4.26	1.26	1.51
3. Energy	19.34	15.31	17.18	11.37
4. Chemicals, Chemical Products and Textiles	11.69	7.75	9.11	8.68
5. Metallic Minerals and Metal Products	3.56	2.22	5.58	2.80
6. Machinery and Equipment	0.62	1.06	1.39	2.16
7. Transportation Equipment	3.25	3.40	3.10	2.03
8. Electrical and Electronic Products	2.10	3.69	1.74	1.69
9. Construction and Related Activities	7.60	7.32	5.79	6.80
10+11. Transportation Services and Communications	0.92	0.90	1.73	1.27
12. Finance and Insurance	25.00	36.14	29.97	33.79
13. Accommodation, Restaurants, Recreation Services and Food Retailing	n.a.	n.a.	n.a.	n.a.
14. Consumer Goods and Services	10.77	4.58	2.91	4.36
15. Other	1.30	0.69	3.06	2.84
Total	100.00	100.00	100.00	100.00

Table 13b
Industrial distribution of Canada's imports from the United Kingdom (percentage)

Industries (SIC-C 1980)	1983	1987	1990	1995
1. Food, Beverage and Tobacco	8.05	5.24	5.00	5.05
2. Wood and Paper	1.38	1.40	1.36	1.46
3. Energy	14.64	40.14	43.22	28.50
4. Chemicals, Chemical Products and Textiles	18.17	10.71	11.32	16.37
5. Metallic Minerals and Metal Products	8.76	7.10	5.43	7.08
6. Machinery and Equipment	17.88	14.48	13.72	13.95
7. Transportation Equipment	13.51	8.39	6.88	10.02
8. Electrical and Electronic Products	5.23	4.74	5.44	11.26
9. Construction and Related Activities	1.89	0.87	0.74	0.78
10. Transportation Services	0.00	0.00	0.00	0.00
11. Communications	2.40	1.74	1.91	1.81
12. Finance and Insurance	0.00	0.00	0.00	0.00
13. Accommodation, Restaurants, Recreation Services and Food Retailing	0.02	0.01	0.16	0.06
14. Consumer Goods and Services	8.08	5.19	4.67	3.62
15. Other	0.00	0.00	0.15	0.03
Total	100.00	100.00	100.00	100.00

Table 14a
Industrial distribution of Canada's inward FDI stock from Japan (percentage)

Industries (SIC-C 1980)	1983	1987	1990	1995
1. Food, Beverage and Tobacco	0.73	0.52	0.73	0.55
2. Wood and Paper	5.36	4.91	21.02	16.30
3. Energy	36.10	22.77	-1.21	3.19
4. Chemicals, Chemical Products and Textiles	0.56	0.79	4.22	4.81
5. Metallic Minerals and Metal Products	4.85	12.25	14.32	13.57
6. Machinery and Equipment	0.96	5.11	5.20	7.28
7. Transportation Equipment	19.80	20.84	14.52	17.65
8. Electrical and Electronic Products	0.68	6.16	5.39	6.07
9. Construction and Related Activities	2.76	0.03	3.41	4.64
10+11. Transportation Services and Communications	0.23	0.36	0.96	0.98
12. Finance and Insurance	8.46	12.35	17.03	13.37
13. Accommodation, Restaurants, Recreation	n.a.	n.a.	n.a.	n.a.
Services and Food Retailing				
14. Consumer Goods and Services	15.45	9.40	7.06	4.43
15. Other	4.06	4.49	7.36	7.15
Total	100.00	100.00	100.00	100.00

Table 14b
Industrial distribution of Canada's imports from Japan (percentage)

Industries (SIC-C 1980)	1983	1987	1990	1995
1. Food, Beverage and Tobacco	1.31	0.99	0.60	0.45
2. Wood and Paper	0.46	0.49	0.35	0.24
3. Energy	0.02	0.11	0.01	0.02
4. Chemicals, Chemical Products and Textiles	5.73	4.70	3.50	3.97
5. Metallic Minerals and Metal Products	7.70	4.30	4.22	4.38
6. Machinery and Equipment	12.76	18.34	14.64	18.35
7. Transportation Equipment	40.07	44.52	46.16	31.02
8. Electrical and Electronic Products	24.79	21.87	24.86	38.14
9. Construction and Related Activities	0.54	0.48	0.46	0.29
10. Transportation Services	0.00	0.00	0.00	0.00
11. Communications	0.24	0.20	0.21	0.15
12. Finance and Insurance	0.00	0.00	0.00	0.00
13. Accommodation, Restaurants, Recreation	0.00	0.00	0.00	0.01
Services and Food Retailing				
14. Consumer Goods and Services	6.37	4.00	4.96	2.99
15. Other	0.00	0.00	0.00	0.00
Total	100.00	100.00	100.00	100.00

Table 15a
Importance of U.S. ownership of FDI stock in Canada (percentage)

Industries (SIC-C 1980)	1983	1987	1990	1995
1. Food, Beverage and Tobacco	77.20	72.70	60.75	58.88
2. Wood and Paper	68.61	46.35	72.11	73.68
3. Energy	75.57	71.74	65.55	56.76
4 Chemicals, Chemical Products and Textiles	81.75	78.58	65.22	71.77
5. Metallic Minerals and Metal Products	84.96	73.23	53.93	64.93
6. Machinery and Equipment	93.59	81.15	76.59	77.54
7. Transportation Equipment	86.28	84.26	80.33	84.68
8. Electrical and Electronic Products	85.10	84.76	83.29	82.85
9. Construction and Related Activities	35.16	56.84	57.49	70.32
10 + 11. Transportation Services and Communications	85.17	85.78	80.96	87.63
12. Finance and Insurance	64.70	51.27	47.90	51.75
13. Accommodation, Restaurants, Recreation Services and Food Retailing	n.a.	n.a.	n.a.	n.a.
14. Consumer Goods and Services	67.25	71.32	69.78	74.66
15. Other	86.96	76.29	63.57	54.81
U.S. FDI as a percentage of all inward FDI	74.94	69.87	64.22	66.97

Table 15b
Importance of U.S. imports into Canada (percentage)

Industries (SIC-C 1980)	1983	1987	1990	1995
1. Food, Beverage and Tobacco	56.07	52.56	55.83	58.63
2. Wood and Paper	79.09	75.28	81.09	87.43
3. Energy	40.07	37.56	29.52	24.76
4. Chemicals, Chemical Products and Textiles	69.73	64.15	69.01	71.44
5. Metallic Minerals and Metal Products	65.36	60.30	67.39	65.84
6. Machinery and Equipment	76.41	64.53	68.22	68.43
7. Transportation Equipment	85.67	81.90	76.87	82.67
8. Electrical and Electronic Products	69.86	66.54	63.47	55.81
9. Construction and Related Activities	65.11	62.18	65.88	61.06
10. Transportation Services	0.00	0.00	0.00	0.00
11. Communications	87.00	83.56	83.51	86.24
12. Finance and Insurance	0.00	0.00	0.00	0.00
13. Accommodation, Restaurants, Recreation Services and Food Retailing	81.47	77.22	72.67	85.38
14. Consumer Goods and Services	31.06	24.16	29.57	39.87
15. Other	0.00	0.00	61.95	66.31
U.S. imports as a percentage of all imports	70.74	67.01	64.52	66.82

Table 16a
Importance of U.K. ownership of FDI stock in Canada (percentage)

Industries (SIC-C 1980)	1983	1987	1990	1995
1. Food, Beverage and Tobacco	16.10	22.27	33.79	21.38
2. Wood and Paper	11.56	10.56	3.01	3.14
3. Energy	7.46	9.71	14.48	9.55
4. Chemicals, Chemical Products and Textiles	10.41	11.19	12.18	7.81
5. Metallic Minerals and Metal Products	5.61	4.98	10.40	4.53
6. Machinery and Equipment	1.64	3.23	4.84	5.05
7. Transportation Equipment	3.77	3.49	4.28	1.85
8. Electrical and Electronic Products	5.25	7.24	4.34	2.34
9. Construction and Related Activities	13.90	14.80	14.97	10.26
10+11. Transportation Services and Communications	5.70	6.10	9.74	4.12
12. Finance and Insurance	18.80	26.26	21.99	18.36
13. Accommodation, Restaurants, Recreation Services and Food Retailing	n.a.	n.a.	n.a.	n.a.
14. Consumer Goods and Services	15.53	13.71	10.43	9.22
15. Other	3.96	2.80	14.97	9.45
U.K. FDI as a percentage of all inward FDI	9.98	11.71	13.13	8.43

Table 16b
Importance of United Kingdom Imports into Canada (percentage)

Industries (SIC-C 1980)	1983	1987	1990	1995
1. Food, Beverage and Tobacco	2.47	2.86	2.69	1.99
2. Wood and Paper	1.23	2.02	1.80	1.22
3. Energy	4.32	26.49	23.24	17.29
4. Chemicals, Chemical Products and Textiles	3.63	3.58	3.43	2.95
5. Metallic Minerals and Metal Products	2.72	3.58	2.44	2.07
6. Machinery and Equipment	3.24	3.91	3.68	2.65
7. Transportation Equipment	1.05	0.93	0.92	0.91
8. Electrical and Electronic Products	1.12	1.49	1.38	1.60
9. Construction and Related Activities	7.28	4.24	3.30	2.91
10. Transportation Services	0.00	0.00	0.00	0.00
11. Communications	3.40	4.89	4.36	3.07
12. Finance and Insurance	0.00	0.00	0.00	0.00
13. Accommodation, Restaurants, Recreation Services and Food Retailing	3.15	4.54	8.63	2.85
14. Consumer Goods and Services	3.55	3.27	2.71	1.58
15. Other	0.00	0.00	14.86	10.32
U.K. imports as a percentage of all imports	2.39	3.71	3.55	2.43

Table 17a
Importance of Japanese ownership of FDI stock in Canada (percentage)

Industries (SIC-C 1980)	1983	1987	1990	1995
1. Food, Beverage and Tobacco	0.29	0.21	0.41	0.23
2. Wood and Paper	2.91	2.83	14.39	13.81
3. Energy	3.11	3.36	-0.29	1.09
4. Chemicals, Chemical Products and Textiles	0.11	0.26	1.62	1.76
5. Metallic Minerals and Metal Products	1.70	6.40	7.66	8.90
6. Machinery and Equipment	0.57	3.63	5.19	6.92
7. Transportation Equipment	5.13	4.99	5.76	6.57
8. Electrical and Electronic Products	0.38	2.82	3.86	3.41
9. Construction and Related Activities	1.13	0.02	2.53	2.85
10+11. Transportation Services and Communications	0.31	0.57	1.55	1.30
12. Finance and Insurance	1.42	2.09	3.59	2.95
13. Accommodation, Restaurants, Recreation Services and Food Retailing	n.a.	n.a.	n.a.	n.a.
14. Consumer Goods and Services	4.97	6.56	7.27	3.81
15. Other	2.77	4.21	10.34	9.67
Japanese FDI as a percentage of all inward FDI	2.22	2.87	3.99	4.06

Table 17b
Importance of Japanese imports into Canada (percentage)

Industries (SIC-C 1980)	1983	1987	1990	1995
1. Food, Beverage and Tobacco	1.06	1.06	0.63	0.39
2. Wood and Paper	1.09	1.39	0.91	0.45
3. Energy	0.02	0.14	0.01	0.03
4. Chemicals, Chemical Products and Textiles	3.03	3.10	2.08	1.60
5. Metallic Minerals and Metal Products	6.32	4.27	3.71	2.85
6. Machinery and Equipment	6.13	9.75	7.67	7.77
7. Transportation Equipment	8.25	9.69	12.03	6.32
8. Electrical and Electronic Products	14.10	13.53	12.30	12.05
9. Construction and Related Activities	5.55	4.65	4.06	2.42
10. Transportation Services	0.00	0.00	0.00	0.00
11. Communications	0.91	1.11	0.93	0.56
12. Finance and Insurance	0.00	0.00	0.00	0.00
13. Accommodation, Restaurants, Recreation Services and Food Retailing	0.23	0.35	0.51	0.84
14. Consumer Goods and Services	7.40	4.96	5.61	2.91
15. Other	0.00	0.00	0.60	1.21
Japanese imports as a percentage of all imports	6.03	6.84	6.99	5.36

Table 18a
Importance of all other countries' ownership of FDI stock in Canada (percentage)

Industries (SIC-C 1980)	1983	1987	1990	1995
1. Food, Beverage and Tobacco	6.41	4.82	5.05	19.51
2. Wood and Paper	16.92	40.25	10.49	9.37
3. Energy	13.87	15.21	20.26	32.60
4. Chemicals, Chemical Products and Textiles	7.73	9.96	20.98	18.67
5. Metallic Minerals and Metal Products	7.73	15.39	28.01	21.64
6. Machinery and Equipment	4.21	11.99	13.38	10.49
7. Transportation Equipment	4.81	7.26	9.63	6.90
8. Electrical and Electronic Products	9.27	5.17	8.52	11.39
9. Construction and Related Activities	49.82	28.35	25.00	16.57
10+11. Transportation Services and Communications	8.82	7.55	7.76	6.95
12. Finance and Insurance	15.09	20.37	26.52	26.94
13. Accommodation, Restaurants, Recreation Services and Food Retailing	n.a.	n.a.	n.a.	n.a.
14. Consumer Goods and Services	12.25	8.41	12.51	12.30
15. Other	6.31	16.70	11.12	26.07
FDI from all other countries as a percentage of all inward FDI	12.86	15.55	18.66	20.54

Table 18b
Importance of all other countries' imports into Canada (percentage)

Industries (SIC-C 1980)	1983	1987	1990	1995
1. Food, Beverage and Tobacco	40.40	43.51	40.85	38.98
2. Wood and Paper	18.58	21.31	16.20	10.91
3. Energy	55.59	35.82	47.23	57.92
4. Chemicals, Chemical Products and Textiles	23.62	29.17	25.48	24.00
5. Metallic Minerals and Metal Products	25.61	31.85	26.46	29.24
6. Machinery and Equipment	14.21	21.81	20.43	21.16
7. Transportation Equipment	5.04	7.49	10.18	10.10
8. Electrical and Electronic Products	14.92	18.44	22.85	30.55
9. Construction and Related Activities	22.06	28.92	26.76	33.60
10. Transportation Services	0.00	0.00	0.00	0.00
11. Communications	8.69	10.45	11.19	10.13
12. Finance and Insurance	0.00	0.00	0.00	0.00
13. Accommodation, Restaurants, Recreation Services and Food Retailing	15.16	17.88	18.19	10.94
14. Consumer Goods and Services	57.99	67.61	62.12	55.64
15. Other	0.00	0.00	22.60	22.16
Imports from all other countries as a percentage of all imports	20.84	22.44	24.94	25.39

4. MODELLING THE LINKS BETWEEN TRADE AND FDI

Firms have several avenues to service foreign markets. The most obvious is of course exports. The costs involved include transportation and related costs such as insurance, tariffs, and exchange rate considerations. We broadly define transfer costs to include all of these costs. FDI is an alternative method of servicing foreign markets. By setting up a foreign production facility, the firm avoids the transfer costs involved in exporting, but incurs the added costs of managing a foreign production facility. In the presence of increasing returns to scale in production, the decision becomes one of trading off scale economies and transfer costs. Obviously, the larger the scale economies, the less likely there will be FDI: if scale economies are large relative to transfer costs, the firm locates all production at home and exports. On the other hand, when scale economies are small relative to transfer costs, it is more likely that the latter will exceed the benefits of centralized production. In short, trade and FDI are substitutes in this scenario. Furthermore, FDI will be horizontal in nature.

In order to analyze the link between trade and FDI, it is not sufficient to simply look at the correlation between trade and FDI. We need to consider a formal model of international trade. International trade is determined by some function of comparative advantage. The three major models of international trade each appeal to a different source of comparative advantage. The monopolistic competition model appeals to increasing returns to scale or product differentiation; the Heckscher-Ohlin model appeals to factor endowments, and the gravity model appeals to transaction costs (broadly defined), as the source of comparative advantage.

It has been shown by Deardorff (1995) that the gravity model can in fact be derived from alternative trade models. That is, the gravity equation is a testable implication of both the Heckscher-Ohlin and monopolistic competition models of international trade. Therefore, using the gravity model as a test for one of these models against the other is misleading because the gravity equation is consistent with both trade models. This is a good reason for us to use the gravity model because we are not concerned in the context of this study with which model is most appropriate to explain Canadian trade. Rather, we would like to simply model links between Canadian outward FDI and exports. We therefore use the gravity model to measure the links between trade and FDI.

The gravity model

The gravity model has been used to explain bilateral trade flows among large groups of countries and over long periods of time (Frankel, Stein and Wei, 1995; Hejazi and Trefler, 1996). We will use the gravity model to explain trade flows between Canada and countries for which bilateral FDI data exist. At the aggregate level, this includes Canada's exports to 33 countries over the period 1970–96. At the industry level, this includes Canada's exports and imports with the United States and the United Kingdom, and imports from Japan over the period 1983–95. The analysis will be extended to take into account FDI as an additional determinant of international trade. Such an analysis will tell us whether there is a relationship between international trade and FDI, after controlling for comparative advantage. The results will indicate empirically whether international trade and FDI are substitutes or complements.

Let t index years, i index the exporting country (Canada), j index the importing country, and let X_{ijt} denote bilateral exports from country i to country j in year t. Let T_{ijt} denote transaction costs broadly defined. The gravity model can therefore be written as follows:

$$\ln(X_{ijt}) \;=\; \alpha \;+\; \ln(T_{ijt})\beta \;+\; 0_{ijt} \qquad (1)$$

The transaction costs variables include (letting *gdp* denote gross domestic product):

Variable	Description	Expected sign in trade regression
gdppc$_{it}$ *gdppc*$_{jt}$	Product of per capita GDPs in countries *i* and *j*	+
gdp$_{it}$ *gdp*$_{jt}$	Product of GDPs in countries *i* and *j*	+
Distance$_{ij}$	A measure of distance between countries *i* and *j*	−
Language$_{ij}$	A dummy variable equal to one if countries *i* and *j* share the same language.	+
Exchange rate	Value of the Canadian dollar in terms of a foreign currency	- for exports + for imports
Dummy variables		
ADJ	Equal to 1 for the United States, 0 otherwise	?
EC	Equal to 1 for EC countries, 0 otherwise	?
East Asia	Equal to 1 for East Asian countries, 0 otherwise	?
Latin America	Equal to 1 for Latin American countries, 0 otherwise	?
APEC	Equal to 1 for APEC countries 0 otherwise	?
Time	A time trend	?

The idea is that countries of similar size and per capita GDP have similar needs both in terms of intermediate inputs (Ethier, 1982) and consumption patterns. Also, trade between two countries should be positively related to the two countries' incomes.[8] In addition, countries that are close together and countries with similar language will have small transaction costs of doing business and correspondingly large levels of bilateral trade. The exchange rate is expected to have an opposite impact in the export and import regressions: a higher exchange rate is expected to increase imports but reduce exports. In addition, we include dummy variables for regional groupings such as the European Community (EC), East Asia (EA), Latin America (LA) and APEC. These variables are meant to measure persistent patterns of trade within regional areas that are not captured by the gravity variables.

Since we are concerned with Canadian exports to other countries, *i* = *C*, denoting Canada:

$$\ln(X_{Cjt}) \ = \ \alpha \ + \ \ln(T_{Cjt})\beta \ + \ 0_{Cjt} \tag{2}$$

The reader familiar with the literature will recognize that, in this section, we are trying to follow as closely as possible the work of Frankel et al. This allows for simple comparisons with previous work. It is recognized, as in Hejazi and Trefler (1996), that the importance of transaction cost motives for trade vary across industries. In other words, the importance of distance and language should vary across industries. The industry level gravity equation is as follows:

$$\ln(X_{Cjgt}) \ = \ \alpha \ + \ \ln(T_{Cjgt})\beta \ + \ 0_{Cjgt} \tag{3}$$

where g denotes industry (or good). Of course, the distance and language variables will not vary by industry, but the dependent variable (exports) will. Also, we still use the aggregate GDP measures rather than industry level output, as data on the latter are not available consistently across countries.

After estimating the gravity model, FDI is added as an additional determinant of trade. This is done at the aggregate level,

$$\ln(X_{Cjt}) \;=\; \alpha \;+\; \ln(T_{Cjt})\beta \;+\; \ln(\mathrm{FDI}_{Cjt})\delta \;+\; 0_{Cjt} \tag{4}$$

and at the industry level,

$$\ln(X_{Cjgt}) \;=\; \alpha \;+\; \ln(T_{Cjgt})\beta \;+\; \ln(\mathrm{FDI}_{Cjgt})\delta \;+\; 0_{Cjgt} \tag{5}$$

Intuitively, FDI fits nicely into the gravity model. According to this model, the source of the comparative advantage is transaction costs, broadly defined. The presence of FDI would indicate that links or networks in the foreign country have already been established, and hence the costs associated with exporting should be lower. As a result, exports should be higher. Therefore, trade and FDI are complementary. We have the necessary data to test this hypothesis.[9,10]

5. ESTIMATION AND INTERPRETATION OF RESULTS

Aggregate regressions

Table 19 presents estimates of the gravity model for exports and outward FDI.[11] In column (i), we have a gravity model that includes the standard gravity variables. Canadian exports are positively related to the product of GDPs, the product of GDPs per capita, and language similarities, but are negatively related to distance between countries and exchange rate. All the gravity variables have the expected sign. The time trend is negative, indicating that Canadian exports have grown less rapidly than the gravity model has predicted.

Column (ii) adds our dummy variables to the regression. Not only are the signs on the initial variables unchanged as a result of this addition, but the coefficient estimates show little variation. The exceptions to this are language, which becomes less important, and exchange rate which becomes more important. The adjacency dummy is positive and statistically significant, indicating Canada trades more with the United States than is predicted by the gravity model. Also positive is the EC, EA, and LA dummies, but the APEC dummy is negative. In column (iii), Canadian outward FDI is added as an additional determinant of exports. Clearly, the coefficient is positive and strongly significant. This indicates that higher Canadian outward FDI increases Canadian exports to that country. In other words, there is a complementary relationship between outward FDI and exports.[12]

Table 20 presents estimates of the gravity model for imports and inward FDI. In column (i), we have a gravity model that includes the standard gravity variables. Canadian imports are positively related to the product of GDPs, the product of GDPs per capita, and language similarities, but are negatively related to distance between countries. The exchange rate has a positive effect on imports, and therefore has the correct sign. The time trend is negative, indicating that imports have grown more slowly than the gravity model has predicted. Column (ii) adds our dummy variables to the regression. Although the signs on the initial variables are unchanged as a result of this addition, the relative importance of GDP, GDP per capita, distance and language increases. The exception is the exchange rate: it is now a negative and statistically insignificant predictor of imports.[13] The adjacency dummy is positive but statistically insignificant. The Latin America and East Asia dummies are strongly positive, whereas both the APEC and the EC dummies are strongly negative. In column (iii), Canadian inward FDI is added as an additional determinant of imports. The coefficient is only one-third the size of the impact of outward FDI on exports, and it is statistically insignificant. In other words, there is no convincing evidence of complementarity on the inward side.

Industry regressions

We have also measured the links between trade and FDI at the industry level. The results are reported in Tables 21 and 22. However, a significant qualification must be expressed about these results: we have not estimated a fully developed model of trade at the industry level. Since we only have bilateral trade and FDI at the industry level on the outward side between Canada and the United States and the United Kingdom, and on the inward side between Canada and the United States, the United Kingdom, and Japan, we cannot use distance, language, and exchange rate variables as there is simply not sufficient variability to identify the independent effects of these variables. In order to use a fully developed gravity model, one would need bilateral data at the industry level at least for the G7 countries and perhaps more. Such data are available from Statistics Canada on a cost recovery basis, and their inclusion in an analysis similar to the one presented in this paper would improve the robustness of the industry level regression results reported here.

Nevertheless, we present some industry level regressions, but use only GDP as the independent variable. That is, we regress exports at the industry level on the product of the two countries' GDPs (Canada and the recipient country) and then, we add FDI as an additional determinant of exports. We do the same for imports. It is immediately apparent that the relationship between trade and FDI varies greatly across industries.

The regression results presented in Tables 21 and 22 are summarized in Table 23. For the export regressions, there is a positive link between exports and outward FDI for 9 industries, but only 3 of these are statistically significant. These 9 industries encompass 58 percent of outward FDI and 66 percent of exports; the 3 industries encompass only 14 percent of outward FDI and 9 percent of exports. There are 4 industries for which there is a negative relationship between exports and outward FDI, and 3 of these are statistically significant. The 4 industries encompass 14 percent of outward FDI and 34 percent of exports; the 3 industries encompass 14 percent of outward FDI and 34 percent of exports.

For the import regressions, there is a positive link between imports and inward FDI for 10 industries, and all are statistically significant. These 10 industries encompass 64 percent of inward FDI and 78 percent of imports. There are 2 industries for which there is a negative relationship between imports and inward FDI, and one of these is statistically significant. The 2 industries encompass 18 percent of inward FDI and 22 percent of imports; the industry showing a significant coefficient encompasses 7 percent of inward FDI and 14 percent of imports.

Therefore, considering only signs but not significance, both on the outward and inward side, there is far more trade and FDI in industries characterized by a complementary relationship than in industries that have a substitutability relationship. These results are consistent with those of the aggregate regressions presented in Tables 20 and 21. However, once we consider the significance of these relationships, we see that on the import side, again far more trade and FDI are in industries characterized by a complementary relationship than in industries that have a substitutability relationship. However, this breaks down on the outward side. Once significance is taken into account, we see that there is only marginally more exports in industries characterized by complementarity, but far less FDI. This latter result is not consistent with the aggregate regressions. It is important to point out that the aggregate regressions include 33 countries whereas the industry level regressions only include a few countries. We therefore put much more weight on the aggregate regressions given the partial nature of the industry level regressions.

Table 19
Gravity model regressions for exports and outward FDI

	Dependent variable: Bilateral exports		
	(i)	(ii)	(iii)
GDP per capita	.505 (8.12)	.548 (9.18)	.506 (8.34)
GDP	.875 (45.62)	.862 (58.28)	.802 (38.24)
Distance	-.364 (-5.28)	-.336 (-4.40)	-.371 (-4.71)
Language	.713 (13.61)	.660 (13.11)	.560 (9.97)
Exchange rates (PPP)	-.222 (-2.21)	-.471 (-4.92)	-.449 (-4.87)
Time	-.046 (-11.41)	-.048 (-13.21)	-.051 (-13.68)
Adjacency		1.58 (10.01)	1.451 (8.92)
European Community		.020 (0.26)	-.043 (-0.56)
East Asia		1.244 (15.67)	1.254 (16.17)
APEC		-.320 (-4.35)	-.351 (-4.85)
Latin America		.691 (9.33)	.607 (7.53)
Outward FDI			.070 (4.55)
Adjusted R^2	.801	.870	.873
Number of observations	810	810	810

Table 20
Gravity model regressions for imports and inward FDI

	Dependent variable: Bilateral imports		
	(i)	(ii)	(iii)
GDP per capita	1.205 (15.43)	1.021 (14.22)	.983 (10.98)
GDP	.785 (37.84)	.815 (46.00)	.797 (29.12)
Distance	-.432 (-5.46)	-.962 (-7.89)	-.974 (-7.83)
Language	.588 (9.41)	.647 (12.70)	.605 (9.82)
Exchange rates (PPP)	.466 (4.58)	-.064 (-0.76)	-.032 (-0.37)
Time	-.034 (-7.96)	-.038 (-9.60)	-.037 (-8.34)
Adjacency		.280 (1.24)	.210 (0.88)
European Community		-.403 (-7.12)	-.409 (-7.48)
East Asia		1.80 (16.62)	1.761 (13.59)
APEC		-.512 (-4.21)	-.467 (-3.29)
Latin America		.598 (5.11)	.570 (4.41)
Inward FDI			.020 (1.10)
Adjusted R^2	.788	.893	.893
Number of observations	694	694	694

Table 21
Industry regressions: Exports and outward FDI

Industry	$EXP = \alpha_0 + \alpha_1\ GDP_C * GDP_i + \varepsilon$			$EXP = \beta_0 + \beta_1\ GDP_C * GDP_i + \beta_2\ FDI + \varepsilon$			
	α_0	α_1	adj R^2	β_0	β_1	β_2	adj R^2
1	-52.68 (-12.30)	1.462 (18.78)	.934	-40.60 (-4.64)	0.989 (3.18)	0.737 (1.57)	.937
2	-56.47 (-18.46)	1.548 (27.83)	.969	-54.19 (-11.34)	1.483 (12.48)	0.073 (0.62)	.968
3	-91.83 (-27.31)	2.18 (35.67)	.981	-79.77 (-9.59)	1.859 (8.75)	0.298 (1.58)	.982
4	-78.69 (-18.78)	1.933 (25.37)	.963	-31.55 (-1.65)	0.940 (2.34)	0.424 (2.51)	.969
5	-49.92 (-23.81)	1.421 (37.27)	.982	-30.78 (-2.36)	0.908 (2.61)	0.473 (1.48)	.983
6	-81.18 (-35.16)	1.971 (46.95)	.989	-80.94 (-36.74)	1.980 (49.17)	-0.045 (-1.86)	.990
7	-140.36 (-28.89)	3.065 (37.43)	.981	-152.50 (-33.24)	3.389 (34.04)	-0.332 (-4.35)	.989
8	-72.86 (-32.37)	1.828 (44.66)	.988	-71.83 (-22.04)	1.801 (24.82)	0.023 (0.44)	.987
9	-78.20 (-12.93)	1.878 (17.08)	.921	-66.21 (-7.27)	1.601 (8.28)	0.179 (1.71)	.927
10	--	--	--	--	--	--	--
11	-93.07 (-37.94)	2.145 (48.07)	.989	-98.81 (-31.34)	2.290 (32.98)	-0.120 (-2.55)	.991
12	--	--	--	--	--	--	--
13	-103.40 (-6.75)	2.276 (8.17)	.733	-51.72 (-3.86)	0.999 (3.49)	1.066 (5.74)	.888
14	-88.83 (-40.97)	2.001 (53.78)	.991	-81.69 (-14.69)	1.954 (16.24)	0.027 (0.41)	.991
15	-47.13 (-6.39)	1.253 (9.37)	.852	-46.78 (-6.00)	1.261 (8.82)	-0.044 (-0.22)	.842

Table 22
Industry regressions: Imports and inward FDI

Industry	$IMP = \alpha_0 + \alpha_1 GDP_C * GDP_i + \varepsilon$			$IMP = \beta_0 + \beta_1 GDP_C * GDP_i + \beta_2 FDI + \varepsilon$			
	α_0	α_1	adj R^2	β_0	β_1	β_2	adj R^2
1	-65.71 (-4.32)	1.678 (6.07)	.485	-53.81 (-9.04)	1.304 (11.82)	0.487 (14.48)	.922
2	-91.19 (-6.66)	2.125 (8.53)	.654	-53.56 (-2.62)	1.254 (2.88)	0.574 (2.38)	.692
3	-2.327 (-0.06)	0.510 (0.76)	-.011	66.973 (4.38)	-1.421 (-4.79)	1.952 (14.33)	.845
4	-64.46 (-6.52)	1.675 (9.32)	.693	-46.39 (-7.04)	1.251 (10.02)	0.295 (7.71)	.881
5	-67.55 (-10.59)	1.726 (14.87)	.853	-45.62 (-5.31)	1.208 (6.56)	0.359 (3.38)	.885
6	-62.74 (-17.69)	1.653 (25.62)	.945	-42.61 (-8.39)	1.211 (11.42)	0.240 (4.76)	.965
7	-102.87 (-24.20)	2.392 (30.94)	.962	-105.17 (-9.10)	2.443 (9.73)	-0.028 (-0.22)	.961
8	-85.75 (-25.23)	2.070 (33.48)	.967	-105.12 (-35.97)	2.503 (41.48)	-0.251 (-8.84)	.989
9	-57.39 (-7.82)	1.500 (11.23)	.772	-50.51 (-8.30)	1.314 (11.46)	0.190 (4.56)	.853
10 + 11	-70.63 (-4.46)	1.746 (6.06)	.485	-7.297 (-0.82)	0.361 (2.07)	0.781 (12.02)	.894
12	--	--	--	--	--	--	--
13	--	--	--	--	--	--	--
14	-48.34 (-12.63)	1.367 (19.64)	.910	-39.12 (-11.27)	1.121 (15.45)	0.241 (5.08)	.946
15	-38.68 (-1.27)	1.081 (1.95)	.114	83.63 (2.92)	-2.109 (-3.22)	2.999 (5.75)	.649

Table 23
Summary of industry level regression results

Export regressions	Number	Percent of outward FDI	Percent of exports
+	9	58.4	65.77
+ and significant	3	14.18	9.36
–	4	14.45	34.23
– and significant	3	13.53	34.22

Import regressions	Number	Percent of inward FDI	Percent of imports
+	10	64.14	77.51
+ and significant	10	64.14	77.51
–	2	17.82	22.48
– and significant	1	7.10	13.92

6. DOMESTIC WELFARE EFFECTS OF OUTWARD FDI

This paper establishes that the critical impact of outward FDI on exports can be answered in a positive way. We show that outward FDI is complementary to exports. This is true at the aggregate level, but not for every industry. Furthermore, we have shown that imports and inward FDI are complementary at the aggregate level, but again not for every industry. An extension of the analysis to more countries may affect the industry level results. Furthermore, at the aggregate level, we have shown that the impact of outward FDI on exports is larger than the impact of inward FDI on imports. In short, Canada's trade balance is expected to increase as a result of higher levels of outward and inward FDI.

We feel that understanding the link between international trade and FDI is a necessary input into the discussion of the associated welfare effects. We have indeed established that outward FDI is strongly associated with export growth, even after other determinants of exports are taken into account. This implies therefore that there is likely to be a positive impact on domestic capital formation and employment. Future work will measure such links more formally. Furthermore, a more detailed industry level analysis would further expand our understanding and would have useful policy implications.

Other important areas to consider include positive income transfers, spillover issues, and tax repercussions. We are able to conclude that the dramatic increase in Canadian outward FDI has had a positive impact on Canadian exports, but we have not linked this to Canadian domestic investment. These higher levels of Canadian outward FDI will also generate larger income payments in the future. Since higher outward FDI stimulates exports and, furthermore, since the impact on exports is larger than the increase in imports resulting from inward FDI, it is likely that domestic employment is also larger as a result of Canada's stronger FDI relationships with the world economy.

CONCLUSIONS

This study has established that international trade and FDI are complements in the Canadian context. That is, over the period 1970–96 and for over 30 countries, we show within a gravity model framework that Canadian outward FDI stimulates domestic exports, and inward FDI stimulates imports. Furthermore, the impact on exports is larger than the impact on imports, indicating that on a net basis, the higher level of openness of Canada to FDI has improved its trade balance.

Data constraints have limited us from undertaking a thorough study at the industry level, but the results we present indicate that there is a great deal of heterogeneity at that level. Some industries are characterized by complementarity while others are characterized by substitutability. At the industry level, there is stronger evidence for a complementary relationship on the inward side than on the outward side. On the outward side, there is no statistically significant link for several industries, but most industries on the inward side show a statistically significant complementary relationship. We also establish that increased levels of openness to FDI in Canada have resulted in higher levels of domestic investment. In other words, increased levels of outward FDI have not been at the expense of domestic investment.

The paper has two clear shortcomings. First, more could be learned about the links between trade and FDI if we could develop a full model of FDI. As the analysis stands, we have specified a full model for trade, but not for FDI. Second, we have not estimated a full gravity model at the industry level because of the small number of countries for which bilateral data are available. Expanding the country coverage would improve the robustness of our results, but would also allow us to measure the impact of increased outward FDI in one industry on trade in other industries. This is especially important if one were to discuss the factor content implications of foreign direct investment and international trade. We plan to undertake work on both of fronts as resources to do so become available.

NOTES

1   Refers to stock throughout this paper, unless flows are specified.

2   The more recent outward stock has been accumulated at higher price levels.

3   See, for example, Safarian (1985) and McFetridge (1991). For studies on the outward side, see Globerman (1994).

4   Such data are available on a cost-recovery basis from Statistics Canada.

5   We provide a review of the theoretical literature in Appendix A.

6   Although 35 countries are listed, we have outward FDI to all countries listed except Saudi Arabia and Israel, and inward FDI from all countries listed except Brazil, Portugal, South Africa, and Indonesia.

7   Obtaining either a longer data set (i.e. 1996) or obtaining additional countries on a bilateral basis is possible, but expensive. Statistics Canada would provide these data on a cost recovery basis.

8   Entering GDP in product form is empirically well established in bilateral trade regressions. It can be justified by the modern theory of trade under imperfect competition. Furthermore, GDP per capita has a positive effect on trade — as countries become more developed, they tend to specialize and trade more. (See Frankel et al., 1995).

9   We could obtain a better understanding of the links between trade and FDI if we could consider and empirically test the formal decision-making process of the firm. It is likely the case that the impact on domestic exports of outward FDI will depend very much on the motivation for the investment. Investments undertaken in services (non-tradeables) are likely to have a positive impact on the Canadian economy: since they are non-tradeables, they do not displace exports. In the absence of the investment, the foreign market would not be serviced. Furthermore, such foreign investments may generate exports of intermediate inputs to the foreign market, thus stimulating domestic investment. Secondly, if the primary motivation for FDI is gaining (regional) market access (tradeables and non-tradeables) then outward FDI can stimulate domestic activity as it stimulates intermediate production. These motivations point to complementarity between outward FDI and exports. Alternatively, FDI may be stimulated by factor endowment differences. In reaction to differences in factor prices, firms may transfer production facilities from Canada to countries that have lower factor costs such as wages. Finally, FDI may be stimulated by the desire to minimize costs based on the trade-off between proximity and concentration. In both cases, the impact on domestic exports is ambiguous. Although these scenarios do stimulate outward FDI at the expense of domestic investment, there is an offsetting effect: exports of intermediates result in an increased demand for domestic production, and therefore capital formation. Unfortunately, there are no (significant) Canadian data on the operations of Canadian MNEs abroad or of foreign MNEs in Canada, making such a fine division of outward FDI infeasible.

10   The gravity model has also been used to explain patterns of FDI (Grosse and Trevino, 1996). Therefore, we could use the gravity model to explain the pattern of Canadian outward FDI, at the aggregate and industry level:

$$\ln(FDI_{Cjt}) \;=\; \alpha \;+\; \ln(T_{Cjt})\beta \;+\; \ln(X_{Cjt})\delta \;+\; 0_{Cjt}$$

and at the industry level:

$$\ln(FDI_{Cjgt}) \;=\; \alpha \;+\; \ln(T_{Cjgt})\beta \;+\; \ln(X_{Cjgt})\delta \;+\; 0_{Cjgt}$$

Those using the gravity model to explain trade flows ignore FDI. Furthermore, those using the gravity model to explain FDI simply condition on trade or ignore trade altogether. Ideally, the interaction or simultaneity between trade and FDI must be considered. Therefore, we can think of estimating an equation for trade and an equation for FDI simultaneously. We do not present estimates for these FDI regressions as they are beyond the scope of this paper.

11   All *t*-statistics reported in this paper use estimated standard errors which are heteroscedastic and autocorrelation consistent.

12   It is important to determine how these results would be affected by taking into account the simultaneity between trade and FDI.

13   Given that the *t*-statistic is small, the coefficient estimate on exchange rates is insignificantly different from zero, and therefore cannot be said to have the wrong sign.

APPENDIX A
THE THEORETICAL LITERATURE[1]

Introduction

FDI theory uses notions of ownership, internalization and location advantages to explain why firms invest in particular countries (see Dunning, 1993, for a review.) Trade theory uses the concept of comparative advantage to describe trade patterns among countries. By adding increasing returns to scale, imperfect competition and product differentiation to the analysis, the new trade theory has been able to explain the growth of intra-industry trade among developed countries (Krugman, 1986).

In order to incorporate FDI into the analysis, the new trade theory relaxes the restrictive assumption that firms are national, which allows firms the opportunity to invest and hence employ factors of production in other countries. Investments can be either vertical or horizontal in nature. Vertical FDI involves the geographical separation of different stages of the production process, whereas horizontal FDI involves an entire duplication of the production process in several countries with the exception of headquarter services. Headquarter services are defined as engineering, managerial and financial services, reputation and trademarks. These services are broadly referred to as R&D and can be transferred to distant production facilities at both no cost and undiminished value.[2] These activities are characterized by increasing returns-to-scale technology. Although the production facilities can be separated from the headquarter activities, the headquarter services are concentrated in one location. Furthermore, the actual production process can be divided into upstream (intermediate goods) production and downstream (final goods) production. All of these activities are characterized by increasing returns to scale.

In such models, firms undertake the headquarter activities in the home market but face three choices for production: undertake all production at home; undertake all production abroad; or produce in both the home and the foreign markets. Once the international distribution of investment is found, trade patterns are more easily derived.

Vertical FDI

Vertical FDI can be motivated by allowing factor proportions to differ across countries (Helpman, 1984; Helpman and Krugman, 1985; Markusen, 1984; Ethier and Horn, 1990). The decision to produce domestically versus internationally can be thought of as a trade-off between transportation costs and scale economies. If there are increasing returns to scale and no transportation costs, then it would be optimal for countries to concentrate production of a product in one location — but the decision on where to locate depends on factor prices. If countries are identical, then there is no FDI, and there is intra-industry trade in differentiated products. The analysis becomes complicated once we allow for asymmetries between countries. When there are small factor-endowment differences, factor price equalization still holds, and there is both inter-industry and intra-industry trade, but the capital abundant country remains a net exporter of the differentiated good and an importer of the homogenous good.

---

[1] This summary of the theoretical literature draws heavily from the *World Investment Report*, UNCTAD, 1996.
[2] We know in practice that this is not the case for transfers to affiliates, and even less so to non-affiliates. See for example, Teece (1977) and Davidson and McFetridge (1984).

When countries are sufficiently different so that factor-price equalization no longer holds, then at least one country will specialize in the good for which it has a comparative advantage. If firms in the differentiated sector are free to invest abroad, they exploit factor-price differences by reallocating headquarter activities to the capital abundant country and plant production to the other. If the factor-endowment differences are not too large, the capital abundant country is still a net exporter of the differentiated good. However, if the differences are large, then the capital abundant country specializes in the production of R&D services which are exported and becomes a net importer of both the differentiated good and the homogenous good. FDI would therefore generate complementary trade flows of finished goods from foreign affiliates to the parent (intra-firm) or the home country (arms length), and there are intra-firm transfers of intangible headquarter services from the parent to the foreign affiliates.

Therefore, factor proportions models would require sufficiently different factor endowments to generate FDI. The implication of such models is that FDI would be greatest among countries that have the widest factor proportions differences, namely developed versus developing. This result is troubling given that most FDI is among developed countries. In this case, factor proportions is likely not the major determinant.

Horizontal FDI

Several studies have integrated horizontal FDI into the theory (Markusen, 1984; Brainard; 1997; Horstman and Markusen, 1992; Markusen and Venables, 1995). Vertical FDI is excluded. Such models, referred to as the proximity-concentration hypothesis, consider the trade-off between plant-level scale economies on the one hand, and firm-level scale economies and transport costs on the other. Firms invest abroad to achieve multi-plant scale economies generated by the high fixed costs of R&D and other headquarter activities (Markusen, 1984). Alternatively, firms invest abroad to overcome transportation costs and geographical and cultural distances between countries. The higher the multi-plant scale economies and transportation costs relative to plant scale economies, the more likely is FDI (Brainard, 1997).

Models based on the trade-off between proximity and concentration postulate a substitution between trade and FDI at both the firm and country levels. Firms either export, or produce and sell locally abroad and transfer intangible headquarter services which do not increase merchandise trade. If factor endowments are identical, then firms can be all national or all transnational, and the coexistence of both occurs only in the case where there is a perfect balance between proximity and concentration advantages. In other words, when countries are identical, there is either intra-industry FDI or intra-industry trade. Furthermore, this theory is successful in explaining FDI among developed countries, but fails in its prediction that FDI should replace trade flows.

The analysis can be further extended to allow for a separation between upstream and downstream production. When a decision is made to invest in a downstream affiliate, intermediates are exported from the parent to the affiliate. This introduces an element of complementarity between horizontal FDI and international trade (Brainard, 1997; Markusen and Venables, 1995) extend the analysis by introducing asymmetries between countries in terms of market size, factor endowments, and technological efficiencies. In such extensions, it is possible for trade and FDI to exist simultaneously. As the disadvantaged countries improve in terms of local market size, factor endowments, and technological efficiency, more and more firms open foreign affiliates in them. Therefore, FDI increases as countries become more similar, contrary to the models which have integrated vertical FDI into the analysis.

Summary

The proximity-concentration hypothesis predicts that firms are more likely to expand production horizontally across borders the higher transport costs and trade barriers and the lower investment barriers and the size of scale economies at the plant level relative to the corporate level. The predictions from the proximity-concentration hypothesis differ from explanations of FDI given in trade theory, namely the factor-proportions hypothesis. The latter theory predicts that firms integrate production vertically across international borders to take advantage of factor price differences which are associated with relative factor supplies.

It is important to add a qualification to all models which rely on the assumption that headquarter type assets are concentrated in the parent, so that multinational firms achieve economies of scale in these by distributing them over production facilities abroad. There is evidence that decentralization of R&D and other headquarter functions has been underway for some time, though more slowly for the United States and Japan than for other home countries. The key resource supplied by the parent then is co-ordination and strategy (Eaton, Lipsey and Safarian, 1994, p. 91-99).

APPENDIX B
THE DATA SET

FDI data

The FDI data were obtained from CANSIM and Statistics Canada. The relevant CANSIM numbers for these FDI data, both at the aggregate and industry levels, are reported in Appendix Tables B–1 and B–2.

Trade data

The export and import data were obtained from CANSIM, and the related CANSIM numbers are reported in Appendix Table B–3. The industry level trade data were obtained from Statistics Canada.

Gravity data

Additional data needed to estimate the gravity model include GDP, population, distance and language dummies. GDP and population data are obtained from the PENN World Tables, and updated using the IMF data tapes. Details on the construction of the PENN data are provided in Summers and Heston (1991). Distance and language dummies have been constructed by Werner Antweiler.

Additional data

Additional data required include price deflators for imports and exports. Canadian imports were deflated using the CANSIM series D14493, D421476 and exports were deflated using D14490, D400466. The Canada-U.S. exchange rate used is the CANSIM series E305100.

Table B–1
CANSIM numbers for aggregate bilateral FDI data
(data availability: 1970 to 1996)

Country	Canadian foreign direct investment abroad	Foreign direct investment in Canada
0 All countries	0 D65201	0 D65212
1 United States	1 D66101	1 D66151
2 Bahamas	2 D66102	2 D66153
3 Bermuda	3 D66103	3 D66152
4 Netherlands Ant.	4 D66104	4 D66154
5 Mexico	5 D66105	5 D66155
6 Brazil	6 D66108	6 n.a.
7 Venezuela	7 D66109	7 D66159
8 Panama	8 D66110	8 D66158
9 United Kingdom	9 D66113	9 D66162
10 Ireland	10 D66114	10 D66169
11 Netherlands	11 D66115	11 D66164
12 Germany	12 D66116	12 D66163
13 Switzerland	13 D66117	13 D66165
14 France	14 D66118	14 D66166
15 Belgium-Luxembourg	15 D66119	15 D66167
16 Greece	16 D66120	16 D66174
17 Spain	17 D66121	17 D66173
18 Italy	18 D66122	18 D66170
19 Portugal	19 D66123	19 n.a.
20 Austria	20 D66124	20 D66171
21 Denmark	21 D66125	21 D66175
22 Norway	22 D66126	22 D66172
23 Sweden	23 D66127	23 D66168
24 South Africa	24 D66130	24 n.a.
25 Singapore	25 D66134	25 D66184
26 Australia	26 D66135	26 D66182
27 Indonesia	27 D66136	27 n.a.
28 Hong Kong	28 D66137	28 D66181
29 Japan	29 D66138	29 D66180
30 Taiwan	30 D66139	30 D66185
31 Malaysia	31 D66140	31 D66186
32 South Korea	32 D66141	32 D66183
33 India	33 D66144	33 D66192
34 Saudi Arabia	34 n.a.	34 D66189
35 Israel	35 n.a.	35 D66190

Table B–2
CANSIM numbers for bilateral FDI data at an industry level
(data availability: 1983 to 1995)

Industries (SIC-C 1980)	Total		United States		United Kingdom		Japan	
	Canadian FDI abroad	Foreign FDI in Canada	Canadian FDI in U.S.	U.S. FDI in Canada	Canadian FDI in U.K.	U.K. FDI in Canada	Canadian FDI in Japan	Japanese FDI in Canada
1. Food, Beverage and Tobacco	D65237	D65270	D65337	D65370	D65437	D65470		D65770
2. Wood and Paper	D65238	D65271	D65338	D65371	D65438	D65471		D65771
3. Energy	D65239	D65272	D65339	D65372	D65439	D65472		D65772
4. Chemicals, Chemical Products and Textiles	D65240	D65273	D65340	D65373	D65440	D65473		D65773
5. Metallic Minerals and Metal Products	D65241	D65274	D65341	D65374	D65441	D65474		D65774
6. Machinery and Equipment	D65242	D65275	D65342	D65375	D65442	D65475		D66575
7. Transportation Equipment	D65243	D65276	D65343	D65376	D65443	D65476		D65776
8. Electrical and Electronic Products	D65244	D65277	D65344	D65377	D65444	D65477		D65777
9. Construction and Related Activities	D65245	D65278	D65345	D65378	D65445	D65478		D65778
10. Transportation Services	D65246	/D65279	D65346	/D65379	D65446	/D65479		/D65779
11. Communications	D65247	D65280	D65347	D65380	D65447	D65480		D65780
12. Finance and Insurance	D65248	n.a.	D65348	n.a.	D65448	n.a.		n.a.
13. Accommodation, Restaurants, Recreation Services and Food Retailing	D65249		D65349		D65449			
14. Consumer Goods and Services	D65250	D65281	D65350	D65381	D65450	D65481		D65781
15. Other	D65251	D65282	D65351	D65382	D65451	D65482		D65782
Total	D65221	D65253	D65321	D65353	D65421	D65453		D65753

Table B–3
CANSIM numbers for aggregate bilateral trade
(data availability: 1970 to 1996)

Country	Canadian exports	Canadian imports	
0 All countries	0 D400466	0 D421476	0 D451000
1 United States	1 D400000	1 D421010	1 D451426
2 Bahamas	2 D400072	2 D421082	2 D451352
3 Bermuda	3 D400069	3 D421079	3 D451354
4 Netherlands Ant.	4 D400024	4 D421034	4 D451382
5 Mexico	5 D400027	5 D421037	5 D451380
6 Brazil	6 D400105	6 D421115	6 D451330
7 Venezuela	7 D400078	7 D421088	7 D451348
8 Panama	8 D400018	8 D421028	8 D451386
9 United Kingdom	9 D400438	9 D421448	9 D451022
10 Ireland	10 D400435	10 D421445	10 D451024
11 Netherlands	11 D400444	11 D421454	11 D451014
12 Germany	12 D400450	12 D421460	12 D451010
13 Switzerland	13 D400396	13 D421406	13 D451052
14 France	14 D400453	14 D421463	14 D451008
15 Belgium-Luxembourg	15 D400442,443,456	15 D421466	15 D451016,018
16 Greece	16 D400414,431	16 D421424,441	16 D451028
17 Spain	17 D400402,427	17 D421412,437	17 D451034
18 Italy	18 D400447	18 D421457	18 D451012
19 Portugal	19 D400405,428	19 D421415,438	19 D451032
20 Austria	20 D400445	20 D421430	20 D451011,042
21 Denmark	21 D400432	21 D421442	21 D451026
22 Norway	22 D400408	22 D421418	22 D451048
23 Sweden	23 D400448	23 D421409	23 D451015,050
24 South Africa	24 D400282	24 D421292	24 D451132
25 Singapore	25 D400183	25 D421193	25 D451236
26 Australia	26 D400138	26 D421148	26 D451276
27 Indonesia	27 D400168	27 D421178	27 D451244
28 Hong Kong	28 D400195	28 D421205	28 D451228
29 Japan	29 D400165	29 D421175	29 D451246
30 Taiwan	30 D400150	30 D421160	30 D451256
31 Malaysia	31 D400189	31 D421199	31 D451232
32 South Korea	32 D400159	32 D421169	32 D451250
33 India	33 D400192	33 D421202	33 D451230
34 Saudi Arabia	34 D400324	34 D421334	34 D451100
35 Israel	35 D400339	35 D421349	35 D451090

APPENDIX C
HOW WELL DO FDI STOCK PROXY FOR FOREIGN SALES

Introduction

One of the compromises made in testing the links between trade and FDI is the assumption that FDI stock is a good proxy for foreign production or foreign sales. This appendix tests how well this assumption works using U.S. FDI and foreign sales.

    a)   How well does U.S. outward FDI proxy for sales by U.S. MNEs operating abroad, both at the aggregate level and in manufacturing?

       Table C-1 provides data on U.S. FDI abroad, both at the aggregate level and in manufacturing. Sales by U.S. affiliates abroad are 3 to 4 times larger than U.S. FDI abroad. This is true for manufacturing as well. We have graphed these in Figure C-1. Graphically, it is quite clear that these series move very much together. The correlation between these variables is also quite high, as is the correlation between their variations.

    b)   How well does U.S. FDI in Canada proxy for sales by U.S. MNEs operating in Canada, both at the aggregate level and in manufacturing?

       Table C–2 provides data on U.S. FDI in Canada, both at the aggregate level and in manufacturing. Sales by U.S. affiliates in Canada are 3 to 4 times larger than U.S. FDI in Canada. This is true for manufacturing as well. We have graphed these in Figure C–2. Graphically, it is quite clear that these series move very much together. The correlation between these variables is also quite high as is the correlation between their variations.

Conclusion

The tables and graphs presented in this appendix indicate quite clearly that FDI and foreign sales are good proxies for one another.

Table C–1
United States outward FDI and sales by U.S. affiliates abroad,
(millions of dollars)

Year	U.S. FDI abroad	Sales by U.S. affiliates abroad	U.S. FDI abroad in manufacturing	Sales by U.S. affiliates abroad in manufacturing
1983	212 150	886 314	83 768	348 450
1984	218 093	898 558	87 331	375 515
1985	238 369	895 460	96 741	387 441
1986	270 472	928 915	108 107	448 399
1987	326 253	1 052 795	135 271	519 619
1988	347 179	1 194 733	142 598	619 293
1989	381 781	1 344 080	147 944	680 231
1990	430 521	1 493 426	170 164	741 169
1991	467 844	1 541 566	179 230	759 686
1992	502 063	1 574 069	186 285	751 993
1993	564 283	1 570 563	192 244	753 023
1994	640 320	1 855 501	211 431	868 945,5
1995	717 554	2 140 438	250 253	984 868

Table C–2
United States outward FDI and sales by U.S. affiliates in Canada,
(millions of dollars)

Year	U.S. FDI in Canada	Sales by U.S. affiliates in Canada	U.S. FDI in Canadian manufacturing	Sales by U.S. affiliates in Canadian manufacturing
1983	44 779	129 674	19 453	63 896
1984	47 498	140 317	21 391	73 623
1985	47 934	138 231	22 306	76 237
1986	52 006	132 488	24 205	75 547
1987	59 145	144 732	27 886	81 084
1988	63 900	168 024	29 763	98 265
1989	63 948	178 713	30 154	99 556
1990	69 508	189 402	33 274	100 847
1991	70 711	188 012	32 042	100 467
1992	68 690	183 844	32 740	98 967
1993	69 922	191 732	33 371	107 614
1994	78 018	211 406,5	36 626	117 542
1995	85 441	231 081	42 215	127 470

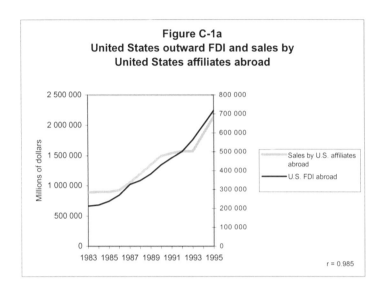

**Figure C-1a
United States outward FDI and sales by
United States affiliates abroad**

r = 0.985

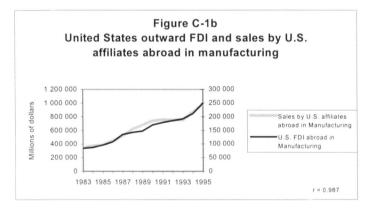

**Figure C-1b
United States outward FDI and sales by U.S.
affiliates abroad in manufacturing**

r = 0.987

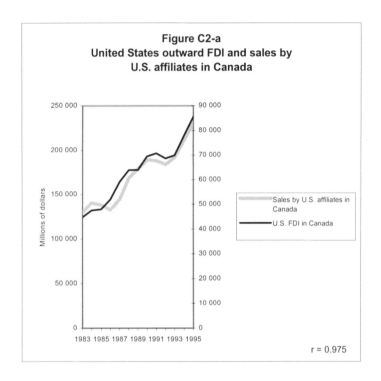

Figure C2-a
United States outward FDI and sales by
U.S. affiliates in Canada

r = 0.975

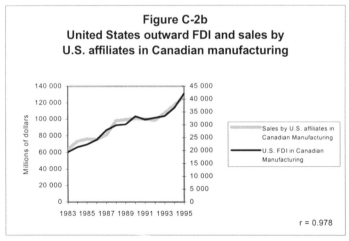

Figure C-2b
United States outward FDI and sales by
U.S. affiliates in Canadian manufacturing

r = 0.978

BIBLIOGRAPHY

Bellak, Christian and John Cantwell (1996). "Foreign Direct Investment - How Much is it Worth? Comment on S. J. Gray and A. M. Rugman." *Transnational Corporations*. 5, 1:85-97.

Blomstrom, Magnus and Ari O. Kokko (1994). "Home Country Effects of Foreign Direct Investment: Sweden." In *Canadian Based Multinational.* Edited by S. Globerman. Industry Canada Research Series. Calgary: The University of Calgary Press.

Blomstrom, Magnus, Robert E. Lipsey and Ksenia Kulchycky (1988). "US and Swedish Direct Investment and Exports." In *Trade Policy Issues and Empirical Analysis.* Edited by R. E. Baldwin. Chicago: University of Chicago Press. p.259-97.

Brainard, S. Lael (1997). "An Empirical Assessment of the Proximity-Concentration Trade-off Between Multinational Sales and Trade." *American Economic Review.*

Caves, Richard (1996). *Multinational Enterprise and Economic Analysis.* Cambridge University Press.

Collins, William J., Kevin H. O'Rourke and Jeffrey G. Williamson (1997). "Were Trade and Factor Mobility Substitutes in History." NBER Working Paper no. 6059.

Davidson, W. H. and D. G. McFetridge (1984). "International Technology Transactions and the Theory of the Firm." *Journal of Industrial Economics*. March: 253-64.

Deardorff, Alan V. (1995). "Determinants of Bilateral Trade: Does Gravity Work in a Neoclassical World." NBER Working Paper no. 5377.

Dunning, John (1993). *Multinational Enterprises and the Global Economy.* Wokingham (England): Addison-Wesley Publishing Co.

Eaton, B. C., R. G. Lipsey and A. E. Safarian (1994). "The Theory of Multinational Plant Location: Agglomerations and Disagglomerations." In *Multinationals in North America.* Edited by L. Eden. The Industry Canada Research Series. Calgary: The University of Calgary Press.

Ethier, Wilfred (1982). "National and International Returns to Scale in the Modern Theory of International Trade." *American Economic Review.* 72: 389-405.

Ethier, Wilfred, and Henrik Horn (1990). "Managerial Control on International Firms and Patterns of Direct Investment." *Journal of International Economics.* 28: 25-45.

Frankel, J. A., Shang-Jin Wei and Ernesto Stein (1995). "APEC and Regional Trading Arrangements in the Pacific." In *Pacific Trade and Investment: Options for the 1990s.* Edited by Wendy Dobson and Frank Flatters. Kingston (Ontario): John Deutsch Institute.

Globerman, S. (ed.) (1994). *Canadian Based Multinationals*. Industry Canada Research Series. Calgary: The University of Calgary Press.

Gray, S. J. and A. Rugman (1994). "Does the United States have a Deficit with Japan in Foreign Direct Investment?" *Transnational Corporations*. 3, 2: 127-37.

Grosse, Robert (1997). "Foreign Direct Investment in Latin America." Thunderbird Business Research Centre Discussion Paper no. 97-4.

Grosse, Robert and Len Trevino (1996). "Foreign Direct Investment in the United States: An Analysis by Country of Origin." *Journal of International Business Studies*. First Quarter.

Graham, Edward M. (1994). "Canadian Direct Investment Abroad and the Canadian Economy: Some Theoretical and Empirical Implications." In *Canadian Based Multinationals*. Edited by S. Globerman. Industry Canada Research Series. Calgary: The University of Calgary Press.

Grubert, Harry and John Mutti (1991). "Taxes, Tariffs, and Transfer Pricing in Multinational Corporate Decision Making." *Review of Economics and Statistics*. May, 73, 2: 285-93.

Gunderson, Morley and Savita Verma (1994). "Labour Market Implications of Outward Foreign Direct Investment." In *Canadian Based Multinationals*. Edited by S. Globerman. Industry Canada Research Series. Calgary: The University of Calgary Press.

Hejazi, Walid and Daniel Trefler (1996). "Canada and the Asia Pacific Region: Views from the Gravity, Monopolistic Competition, and Heckscher-Ohlin Models." In *The Asia Pacific Region and the Global Economy: A Canadian Perspective*. Edited by Richard Harris. Industry Canada Research Series. Calgary: The University of Calgary Press.

Helpman, Elhanan (1984). "A Simple Theory of International Trade with Multinational Corporations." *Journal of Political Economy*. 93, 2: 451-71.

Helpman, Elhanan and Paul Krugman (1985). *Market Structure and Foreign Trade*. Cambridge (MA): MIT Press.

Horst, Thomas (1972). "The Industrial Composition of US Exports and Subsidiary Sales to the Canadian Market." *American Economic Review*. 62, 1: 37-45.

Horstman, Ignatius and James Markusen (1992). "Endogenous Market Structures in International Trade." *Journal of International Economics*. 32, February: 109-29.

Hufbauer, G. C. and M. Adler (1968). "US Manufacturing Investment and the Balance of Payments." Tax Policy Research Study Number 1. Washington (DC): US Treasury Department.

Jun, Kwang W. and Harinder Singh (1996). "The Determinants of Foreign Direct Investment in Developing Countries." *Transnational Corporations*. 5, 2: 67-105.

Krugman, Paul R. (1986). "Intra-industry Specialization and the Gains from Trade." *Journal of Political Economy*. 89: 959-73.

Lipsey, Robert E. and Merle Yahr Weiss (1984). "Foreign Production and Exports of Individual Firms." *The Review of Economics and Statistics*. p. 304-8.

Markusen, J. R. (1984). "Multinationals, Multi-Plant Economics, and the Gains from Trade." *Journal of International Economics*. 16, May: 205-26.

Markusen, J. R. and Anthony J. Venables (1995). "The Increased Importance of Multinationals in North American Economic Relationships: A Convergence Hypothesis." In *The New Transatlantic Economy*. Edited by Mathew W . Canzoneri, Wilfred J. Ethier and Victoria Grilli. London: Cambridge University Press.

McFetridge, D. G. (1991). "Introduction." In *Foreign Investment, Technology, and Economic Growth*. Edited by D. G. McFetridge. Investment Canada Research Series. Calgary: The University of Calgary Press.

Pfaffermayr, M. (1994). "Foreign Direct Investment and Exports: A Time Series Approach." *Applied Economics*. 26: 337-51.

Rao, Someshwar, Ashfaq Ahmad, and Colleen Barnes (1996). "Foreign Direct Investment and APEC Economic Integration." Industry Canada Working Paper Series no 8.

Rao, Someshwar, Ashfaq Ahmad and Marc Legault (1994). "Canadian-Based Multinationals: An Analysis of Activities and Performance." *Canadian Based Multinationals*. Edited by S. Globerman. Industry Canada Research Series. Calgary: The University of Calgary Press.

Safarian, A. E. (1985). "Foreign Direct Investment: A Survey of Canadian Reserarch." Montreal: The Institute for Research on Public Policy.

Summers, Robert and Alan Heston (1991). "The Penn World Tables (Mark 5): An Expanded Set of International Comparisons, 1950-1988." *Quarterly Journal of Economics*. 106: 327-68.

Teece, D. J. (1977). "Technology Transfer by Multinational Firms: The Resource Cost of Transferring Technological Know-how." *Economic Journal*. 87: 242-61.

UNCTAD. World Investment Report. Various issues.

US Department of Commerce (1995). "Foreign Direct Investment in the United States: Detail for Historical-Cost Position and Related Capital and Income Flows." *Survey of Current Business*. August: 53-78.

INDUSTRY CANADA RESEARCH PUBLICATIONS

INDUSTRY CANADA WORKING PAPER SERIES

No. 1 **Economic Integration in North America: Trends in Foreign Direct Investment and the Top 1,000 Firms**, Industry Canada, Micro-Economic Policy Analysis Staff including John Knubley, Marc Legault and P. Someshwar Rao, 1994.

No. 2 **Canadian-Based Multinationals: An Analysis of Activities and Performance**, Industry Canada, Micro-Economic Policy Analysis Staff including P. Someshwar Rao, Marc Legault and Ashfaq Ahmad, 1994.

No. 3 **International R&D Spillovers Between Industries in Canada and the United States**, Jeffrey I. Bernstein, Carleton University and National Bureau of Economic Research, under contract with Industry Canada, 1994.

No. 4 **The Economic Impact of Mergers and Acquisitions on Corporations**, Gilles Mcdougall, Micro-Economic Policy Analysis, Industry Canada, 1995.

No. 5 **Steppin' Out: An Analysis of Recent Graduates Into the Labour Market**, Ross Finnie, School of Public Administration, Carleton University and Statistics Canada, 1995.

No. 6 **Measuring the Compliance Cost of Tax Expenditures: The Case of Research and Development Incentives**, Sally Gunz, University of Waterloo, Alan Macnaughton, University of Waterloo, and Karen Wensley, Ernst & Young, Toronto, under contract with Industry Canada, 1996.

No. 7 **Governance Structure, Corporate Decision-Making and Firm Performance in North America**, P. Someshwar Rao and Clifton R. Lee-Sing, Micro-Economic Policy Analysis, Industry Canada, 1996.

No. 8 **Foreign Direct Investment and APEC Economic Integration**, Ashfaq Ahmad, P. Someshwar Rao and Colleen Barnes, Micro-Economic Policy Analysis, Industry Canada, 1996.

No. 9 **World Mandate Strategies for Canadian Subsidiaries**, Julian Birkinshaw, Institute of International Business, Stockholm School of Economics, under contract with Industry Canada, 1996.

No. 10 **R&D Productivity Growth in Canadian Communications Equipment and Manufacturing**, Jeffrey I. Bernstein, Carleton University and National Bureau of Economic Research, under contract with Industry Canada, 1996.

No. 11 **Long-run Perspective on Canadian Regional Convergence**, Serge Coulombe, Department of Economics, University of Ottawa, and Frank C. Lee, Industry Canada, 1996.

No. 12 **Implications of Technology and Imports on Employment and Wages in Canada**, Frank C. Lee, Industry Canada, 1996.

No. 13 **The Development of Strategic Alliances in Canadian Industries: A Micro Analysis,** Sunder Magun, Applied International Economics, 1996.

No. 14 **Employment Performance in the Knowledge-Based Economy**, Surendra Gera, Industry Canada, and Philippe Massé, Human Resources Development Canada, 1996.

No. 15 **The Knowledge-Based Economy: Shifts in Industrial Output**, Surendra Gera, Industry Canada, and Kurt Mang, Department of Finance, 1997.

No. 16 **Business Strategies of SMEs and Large Firms in Canada**, Gilles Mcdougall and David Swimmer, Micro-Economic Policy Analysis, Industry Canada, 1997.

No. 17 **Impact of China's Trade and Foreign Investment Reforms on the World Economy**, Winnie Lam, Micro-Economic Policy Analysis, Industry Canada, 1997.

No. 18 **Regional Disparities in Canada: Characterization, Trends and Lessons for Economic Policy**, Serge Coulombe, Department of Economics, University of Ottawa, 1997.

No. 19   **Inter-Industry and U.S. R&D Spillovers, Canadian Industrial Production and Productivity Growth,** Jeffrey I. Bernstein, Carleton University and National Bureau of Economic Research, under contract with Industry Canada, 1998.

No. 20   **Information Technology and Labour Productivity Growth: An Empirical Analysis for Canada and the United States,** Surendra Gera, Wulong Gu and Frank C. Lee, Micro-Economic Policy Analysis, Industry Canada, 1998.

No. 21   **Capital-Embodied Technical Change and the Productivity Growth Slowdown in Canada,** Surendra Gera, Wulong Gu and Frank C. Lee, Micro-Economic Policy Analysis, Industry Canada, 1998.

No. 22   **The Corporate Tax Structure and the Effects on Production, Cost and Efficiency,** Jeffrey I. Bernstein, Carleton University and National Bureau of Economic Research, under contract with Industry Canada, 1998.

No. 23   **Restructuring in Canadian Industries: A Micro Analysis,** Sunder Magun, Applied International Economics, under contract with Industry Canada, 1998.

No. 24   **Canadian Government Policies Toward Inward Foreign Direct Investment,** Steven Globerman, Simon Fraser University and Western Washington University, and Daniel Shapiro, Simon Fraser University, under contract with Industry Canada, 1998.

No. 25   **A Structuralist Assessment of Technology Policies – Taking Schumpeter Seriously on Policy,** Richard G. Lipsey and Kenneth Carlaw, Simon Fraser University, with a contribution by Davit D. Akman, research associate, under contract with Industry Canada, 1998.

No. 26   **Intrafirm Trade of Canadian-Based Foreign Transnational Companies,** Richard A. Cameron, Micro-Economic Policy Analysis, Industry Canada, 1998.

No. 27   **Recent Jumps in Patenting Activities: Comparative Innovative Performance of Major Industrial Countries, Patterns and Explanations,** Mohammed Rafiquzzaman and Lori Whewell, Micro-Economic Policy Analysis, Industry Canada, 1998.

No. 28   **Technology and the Demand for Skills: An Industry-Level Analysis,** Surendra Gera and Wulong Gu, Industry Canada, and Zhengxi Lin, Statistics Canada, 1999.

No. 29   **The Productivity Gap Between Canadian and U.S. Firms,** Frank Chung Lee and Jianmin Tang, Micro-Economic Policy Analysis, Industry Canada, 1999.

No. 30   **Foreign Direct Investment and Productivity Growth: The Canadian Host-Country Experience,** Surendra Gera, Wulong Gu and Frank C. Lee, Micro-Economic Policy Analysis, Industry Canada, 1999.

INDUSTRY CANADA DISCUSSION PAPER SERIES

No. 1   **Multinationals as Agents of Change: Setting a New Canadian Policy on Foreign Direct Investment,** Lorraine Eden, Carleton University, 1994.

No. 2   **Technological Change and International Economic Institutions,** Sylvia Ostry, Centre for International Studies, University of Toronto, under contract with Industry Canada, 1995.

No. 3   **Canadian Corporate Governance: Policy Options,** Ronald. J. Daniels, Faculty of Law, University of Toronto, and Randall Morck, Faculty of Business, University of Alberta, 1996.

No. 4   **Foreign Direct Investment and Market Framework Policies: Reducing Frictions in APEC Policies on Competition and Intellectual Property,** Ronald Hirshhorn, 1996.

No. 5   **Industry Canada's Foreign Investment Research: Messages and Policy Implications,** Ronald Hirshhorn, 1997.

No. 6   **International Market Contestability and the New Issues at the World Trade Organization,** Edward M. Graham, Institute for International Economics, Washington (DC), under contract with Industry Canada, 1998.

INDUSTRY CANADA OCCASIONAL PAPER SERIES

No. 1   **Formal and Informal Investment Barriers in the G-7 Countries: The Country Chapters**, Industry Canada, Micro-Economic Policy Analysis Staff including Ashfaq Ahmad, Colleen Barnes, John Knubley, Rosemary D. MacDonald and Christopher Wilkie, 1994.

Formal and Informal Investment Barriers in the G-7 Countries: Summary and Conclusions, Industry Canada, Micro-Economic Policy Analysis Staff including Ashfaq Ahmad, Colleen Barnes and John Knubley, 1994.

No. 2   **Business Development Initiatives of Multinational Subsidiaries in Canada**, Julian Birkinshaw, University of Western Ontario, under contract with Industry Canada, 1995.

No. 3   **The Role of R&D Consortia in Technology Development**, Vinod Kumar, Research Centre for Technology Management, Carleton University, and Sunder Magun, Centre for Trade Policy and Law, University of Ottawa and Carleton University, under contract with Industry Canada, 1995.

No. 4   **Gender Tracking in University Programs**, Sid Gilbert, University of Guelph, and Alan Pomfret, King's College, University of Western Ontario, 1995.

No. 5   **Competitiveness: Concepts and Measures**, Donald G. McFetridge, Department of Economics, Carleton University, 1995.

No. 6   **Institutional Aspects of R&D Tax Incentives: The SR&ED Tax Credit**, G. Bruce Doern, School of Public Administration, Carleton University, 1995.

No. 7   **Competition Policy as a Dimension of Economic Policy: A Comparative Perspective**, Robert D. Anderson and S. Dev Khosla, Economics and International Affairs Branch, Bureau of Competition Policy, Industry Canada, 1995.

No. 8   **Mechanisms and Practices for the Assessment of The Social and Cultural Implications of Science and Technology**, Liora Salter, Osgoode Hall Law School, University of Toronto, under contract with Industry Canada, 1995.

No. 9   **Science and Technology: Perspectives for Public Policy**, Donald G. McFetridge, Department of Economics, Carleton University, under contract with Industry Canada, 1995.

No. 10   **Endogenous Innovation and Growth: Implications for Canada**, Pierre Fortin, Université du Québec à Montréal and the Canadian Institute for Advanced Research, and Elhanan Helpman, Tel Aviv University and the Canadian Institute for Advanced Research, under contract with Industry Canada, 1995.

No. 11   **The University-Industry Relationship in Science and Technology**, Jérôme Doutriaux, University of Ottawa, and Margaret Barker, Meg Barker Consulting, under contract with Industry Canada, 1995.

No. 12   **Technology and the Economy: A Review of Some Critical Relationships**, Michael Gibbons, University of Sussex, under contract with Industry Canada, 1995.

No. 13   **Management Skills Development in Canada**, Keith Newton, Industry Canada, 1995.

No. 14   **The Human Factor in Firm's Performance: Management Strategies for Productivity and Competitiveness in the Knowledge-Based Economy**, Keith Newton, Industry Canada, 1996.

No. 15   **Payroll Taxation and Employment: A Literature Survey**, Joni Baran, Industry Canada, 1996.

No. 16   **Sustainable Development: Concepts, Measures, Market and Policy Failures at the Open Economy, Industry and Firm Levels**, Philippe Crabbé, Institute for Research on the Environment and Economy, University of Ottawa, 1997.

No. 17   **Measuring Sustainable Development: A Review of Current Practice**, Peter Hardi and Stephan Barg, with Tony Hodge and Laszlo Pinter, International Institute for Sustainable Development, 1997.

No. 18   **Reducing Regulatory Barriers to Trade: Lessons for Canada from the European Experience**, Ramesh Chaitoo and Michael Hart, Center for Trade Policy and Law, Carleton University, 1997.

No. 19   **Analysis of International Trade Dispute Settlement Mechanisms and Implications for Canada's Agreement on Internal Trade**, E. Wayne Clendenning and Robert J. Clendenning, E. Wayne Clendenning & Associates Inc., under contract with Industry Canada, 1997.

No. 20   **Aboriginal Businesses: Characteristics and Strategies for Growth**, David Caldwell and Pamela Hunt, Management Consulting Centre, under contract with Aboriginal Business Canada, Industry Canada, 1998.

CANADA IN THE 21ST CENTURY SERIES

No. 1   **Global Trends: 1980-2015 and Beyond**, J. Bradford De Long, University of California, Berkeley, under contract with Industry Canada, 1998.

No. 2   **Broad Liberalization Based on Fundamentals: A Framework for Canadian Commercial Policy**, Randy Wigle, Wilfrid Laurier University, under contract with Industry Canada, 1998.

No. 3   **North American Economic Integration: 25 Years Backward and Forward**, Gary C. Hufbauer and Jeffrey J. Schott, Institute for International Economics, Washington (DC), under contract with Industry Canada, 1998.

No. 4   **Demographic Trends in Canada, 1996-2006 : Implications for the Public and Private Sectors**, David K. Foot, Richard A. Loreto and Thomas W. McCormack, Madison Avenue Demographics Group, under contract with Industry Canada, 1998.

No. 5   **Capital Investment Challenges in Canada**, Ronald P. M. Giammarino, University of British Columbia, under contract with Industry Canada, 1998.

No. 6   **Looking to the 21st Century – Infrastructure Investments for Economic Growth and for the Welfare and Well-Being of Canadians**, Christian DeBresson, Université du Québec à Montréal, and Stéphanie Barker, Université de Montréal, under contract with Industry Canada, 1998.

No. 7   **The Implications of Technological Change for Human Resource Policy**, Julian R. Betts, University of California, San Diego, under contract with Industry Canada, 1998.

No. 8   **Economics and the Environment: The Recent Canadian Experience and Prospects for the Future**, Brian R. Copeland, University of British Columbia, under contract with Industry Canada, 1998.

No. 9   **Individual Responses to Changes in the Canadian Labour Market**, Paul Beaudry and David A. Green, University of British Columbia, under contract with Industry Canada, 1998.

No. 10   **The Corporate Response – Innovation in the Information Age**, Randall Morck, University of Alberta, and Bernard Yeung, University of Michigan, under contract with Industry Canada, 1998.

No. 11   **Institutions and Growth: Framework Policy as a Tool of Competitive Advantage for Canada**, Ronald J. Daniels, University of Toronto, under contract with Industry Canada, 1998.

PERSPECTIVES ON NORTH AMERICAN FREE TRADE SERIES

No. 1   **Can Small-Country Manufacturing Survive Trade Liberalization? Evidence from the Canada–U.S. Free Trade Agreement**, Keith Head and John Ries, University of British Columbia, under contract with Industry Canada, 1999.

No. 2   **Modelling Links Between Canadian Trade and Foreign Direct Investment**, W. Hejazi and A.E. Safarian, University of Toronto, under contract with Industry Canada, 1999.

JOINT PUBLICATIONS

Capital Budgeting in the Public Sector, in collaboration with the John Deutsch Institute, Jack Mintz and Ross S. Preston eds., 1994.

Infrastructure and Competitiveness, in collaboration with the John Deutsch Institute, Jack Mintz and Ross S. Preston eds., 1994.

Getting the Green Light: Environmental Regulation and Investment in Canada, in collaboration with the C.D. Howe Institute, Jamie Benidickson, G. Bruce Doern and Nancy Olewiler, 1994.

To obtain copies of documents published under the Research Publications Program, please contact:

Publications Officer
Micro-Economic Policy Analysis
Industry Canada
5th Floor, West Tower
235 Queen Street
Ottawa, Ontario, K1A 0H5

Tel.: (613) 952-5704
Fax: (613) 991-1261
E-mail: mepa.apme@ic.gc.ca